LITERARY MASTERS

ISSN 1526-1530

LITERARY MASTERS

Volume 2

Ernest Hemingway

Michael Reynolds

A MANLY, INC. BOOK

Detroit
San Francisco
London
Boston
Woodbridge, CT

ERNEST HEMINGWAY

Matthew J. Bruccoli and Richard Layman, *Editorial Directors*

ISBN 0-7876-3961-3

ISSN 1526-1530

Printed in the United States of America

10 9 8 7 6 5 4 3 2 1

TABLE OF CONTENTS

A NOTE TO THE READER

THE TELLER IN THE TALE

by Alvin Kernan,
Andrew W. Mellon
Foundation

A few years ago it was fashionable to speak of "the death of the author" and to argue that "language writes, not the man." These post-modernist views were part of a philosophy that discounted the individuality of the writer in favor of a world of impersonal texts and systems, such as language, which furnish a "scriptor" with the only conceptions of reality he or she can have. In this view of things the author disappeared into a "mere grammatical subject"; the time and place were doing the writing, not the author.

This vast, gray, impersonal view has not prevailed, however, because it goes against the grain of what we all know and feel to be the actual case. Historically, our literature is not just a set of coded texts but living writings intertwined with the names of the men and women who wrote them. We cannot think of *The Canterbury Tales* without thinking of the sly but somewhat bumbling Geoffrey Chaucer, good-natured but sharply ironic, who introduces himself as one of the pilgrims in his own poem. And we try our best to see William Shakespeare, always a somewhat mysterious fellow, in the figure of the magician Prospero on his magic island in *The Tempest*. Charles Dickens, as a frightened boy sent to work in the blacking factory in industrialized London, hangs about his novels in the same way that Ernest Hemingway in his macho pose and his death by suicide is always present when we turn the pages of *A Farewell to Arms* or the "Up in Michigan" stories. As in the last example, the lives of the poets often throw dark shadows back on their works. The alcoholic F. Scott Fitzgerald ends his life trying desperately to write another novel as good as his early *The Great Gatsby*. Flannery O'Connor sits in her small house in Georgia, suffering from a disease—lupus—that ravages her immune system, and records experiences of Americans who are as vulnerable to the world as is her own body.

The teller not only writes the tale, but, in doing so, he or she becomes a part of it; and our sense of the tale is not complete until the teller's presence is evoked. This is one reason why biographies and vignettes, collections of biographical information, and memories of the type found in these volumes about our writers are so interesting and so useful. More than useful, really. We have not fully read the tale until we can see the teller in it, who will, if we come to know him or her well enough, sensitize us to how the tale is told and what is likely to be in it. Every tale-teller has a distinctive way of telling—the style—and a particular subject matter. To know who is writing is, therefore, to know to look for things that would otherwise escape us. Theodore Dreiser, the American novelist, was a moody man, pessimistic about the possibilities of life, convinced that our fates are woven from a host of small details, the need for a winter coat in *Sister Carrie* or the bright attractiveness of an upper middle-class parlor in *An American Tragedy*. These ordinary details can in their bulk bore us and turn us away from the story if we are not aware that this is the Dreiserian signature, the way in which he renders the flatness of ordinary life and points to the fate that lies concealed in it.

Every author differs from every other in how and what he or she writes, but in the end they combine, if we see and know them well enough, to create a scene that is close to the center of literature, to its place and role in the world. Some writing careers portray this scene more powerfully than others do. Samuel Johnson, for example, was a personality so titanic as nearly to overwhelm his writings, physically grotesque, frequently nearly mad with depression, an impoverished hack most of his life, endlessly talking for victory and heroically facing the hard facts of human life. In Johnson's life, writing his great dictionary of the English language or his *Lives of the Poets* was his defense against the madness of emptiness and meaninglessness. That is to say, he wrote to preserve his sanity by giving order and meaning to the world and to the language through which we approach it.

Every teller of tales, when we come to know him or her, is engaged in something like this Johnsonian struggle to order and make sense of the world of random facts and experiences, to preserve some sense of things, people, and times that would otherwise be forgotten and lost forever in the past. Consider another writer, our own Southern novelist William Faulkner, a struggler who is not as successful as Johnson in his authorial task of imposing order on a messy and painful sense of the confusions of life. Faulkner's story is that of a mythical Mississippi county, Yoknapatawpha County, that he creates in an attempt to locate and order in time and space the confused and confusing memories of the Southern past, such as the Civil War and slavery and primitive wilderness, with modern-day consciousness that cannot forget the past but also cannot reconcile it with its own immediate interests and thoughts. The strain shows in Faulkner's stories, in the absence of clear chronology, in the tangled syntax of his long sentences, in his frequent descent into stream-of-consciousness writing.

To include the tellers with their tales, which is what this series of the Gale Study Guides is designed to make possible for the common reader, is to see the heroic scene of literature itself, throughout the world, where men and women writers make and have made the most skillful use of the word-hoard of language and the freedom of fiction to preserve our collective past and to make sense out of things that in their multitude are always threatening to fly apart into chaos.

ACKNOWLEDGMENTS

This book was produced by Bruccoli Clark Layman, Inc. R. Bland Lawson is the series editor and the in-house editor.

Production manager is Philip B. Dematteis.

Copyediting supervisor is Phyllis A. Avant. Senior copyeditor is Thom Harman. The copyediting staff includes Brenda Carol Blanton, James Denton, Worthy B. Evans, Melissa D. Hinton, William Tobias Mathes, and Jennifer Reid.

Indexing specialist is Alex Snead.

Layout and graphics supervisor is Janet E. Hill. Graphics staff includes Karla Corley Brown and Zoe R. Cook.

Photography editors are Charles Mims, Scott Nemzek, Alison Smith, and Paul Talbot. Digital photographic copy work was performed by Joseph M. Bruccoli.

Systems manager is Marie L. Parker.

Typesetting Supervisor is Kathleen M. Flanagan. The typesetting staff includes Mark J. McEwan, Kimberly Kelly, and Patricia Flanagan Salisbury.

COPYRIGHTED PHOTOGRAPHY

Following is a list of the copyright holders who have granted us permission to reproduce material in this volume of Gale Study Guides to Great Literature. Every effort has been made to trace copyright, but if omissions have been made, please let us know.

COPYRIGHTED MATERIAL IN *Literary Masters, Volume 2: Ernest Hemingway* IS REPRODUCED FROM THE FOLLOWING PERIODICALS:

The New York Times, 11 August 1940; 17 September 1950. Copyright 1940, 1950 by The New York Times Company. Both reproduced by permission. 3 July 1961; 16 July 1961; 12 January 1992. Copyright ©

Hemingway, Ernest, in Italian uniform, 1918. John F. Kennedy Library.

Hemingway, Ernest, John Dos Passos, Gerald Murphy, and an Austrian ski instructor, full length, photograph. John F. Kennedy Library.

Hemingway, Ernest, kneeling with kill in Africa, 1937, photograph. Archive Photos, Inc. Reproduced by permission.

Hemingway, Ernest, Lady Duff Twysden, Hadley, Donald Ogden Steward, and Pat Guthrie sitting at a sidewalk café, Spain, 1925, photograph. John F. Kennedy Library.

Hemingway, Ernest, steers his fishing boat, *Pilar*, out into the Gulf Stream, photograph. John F. Kennedy Library.

Hemingway, Ernest, unshaven, head and shoulders, photograph. © C. M. Zoehrer. John F. Kennedy Library.

Hemingway, Ernest, wearing hat and coat, photograph. AP/Wide World Photos. Reproduced by permission.

Hemingway, Jack, Spencer Tracy, Ernest Hemingway, and Mary Hemingway in a corner of the Floridita, Havana. John F. Kennedy Library.

Hemingway, Marcelline, Clarence Edmonds Hemingway, Madelaine Hemingway, Grace Hall Hemingway, Ursula Hemingway, and Ernest Miller Hemingway, portrait. John F. Kennedy Library.

Welsh, Mary, hunting, photograph. Archive Photos, Inc. Reproduced by permission.

CHRONOLOGY OF EVENTS IN
ERNEST HEMINGWAY'S LIFE

In the last year of the nineteenth century, Ernest Hemingway was born in the afterglow of the Spanish-American War. Nothing about his birth or his parentage was particularly significant. Sixty-one years and eleven months later, when he died by his own hand, it was headline news in almost every major newspaper in the world. He had become an American icon, a face so familiar that it needed no identifying caption. In the last year of the twentieth century, the centennial of his birth, the world once more paid homage to this American writer who changed the way Americans wrote about themselves.

As one of his sons has said, Hemingway lived on a fast clock. He burned with an intensity that made emotional and physical demands both on himself and those around him. In the first half of the twentieth century, he was present at the crucial events that shaped world history. In World War I, he was wounded on the Italian front, a fitting initiation into the violence that would characterize his times. As a journalist, he covered the Greco-Turkish War in 1922, the Spanish Civil War from 1937 to 1939, and World War II in 1940 and 1944. As a serious student of revolutions, he observed political intrigues in Spain, Cuba, and the Dominican Republic. As a writer, he published books in every decade from the 1920s to the 1990s, five of them from the grave. He won prestigious literary prizes, sat down at table in the Franklin Roosevelt White House, and was invited to the John F. Kennedy inauguration. He was born before the Wright brothers got their fledgling airplane off the ground and lived long enough to see satellites circling the globe. Before he died, Hemingway left a shelf of novels, nonfiction, and letters that provide a natural history of how human beings behaved in his time. It is a cautionary tale at best, frequently sad, an ongoing lesson in loss and how to face it.

1899: In Oak Park, Illinois, Ernest Hemingway is born on 21 July, the second child of Clarence Edmonds and Grace Hall Hemingway.

The Hemingway family, ca. 1906. Left to right: Marcelline, age 10; Dr. Clarence Edmonds Hemingway, age 35; on his lap, Madelaine, age 1 1/2; Grace Hall Hemingway, age 34; on her lap, Ursula, age 4; and Ernest Miller Hemingway, age 9. Here Marcelline and Ernest are still wearing their hair in Dutch bobs at their mother's insistence on treating them as twins.

1905–1913: Ernest and his older sister, Marcelline, attend grade school in Oak Park. Each summer of his youth, Hemingway spends two months on the lower Michigan peninsula at the family cottage on Walloon Lake, which will later become the setting for many of the Nick Adams stories.

1913–1917: Ernest and Marcelline attend Oak Park and River Forest High School, where he is a mediocre athlete but a steady contributor to the school newspaper and literary magazine during his last two years. In August 1914, before his sophomore year, World War I begins in Europe. In April 1917, as Ernest prepares to graduate, the United States declares war on the side of England, France, and Italy. That October he moves to Kansas City, Missouri, to take a job as cub reporter on *The Kansas City Star*.

1918: In the spring Hemingway enlists with the American Red Cross to become an ambulance driver on the Italian front. In June he is assigned to the Red Cross's Section Four, stationed at Schio, Italy. On 8 July, while delivering chocolate to frontline troops at Fossalta, Hemingway is wounded by an Austrian trench-mortar canister. From July to December he is in the Milan Red Cross hospital for an operation to rebuild his right knee and a lengthy process of physical rehabilitation. He falls in love with his nurse, Agnes Von Kurowsky, eight years his senior.

1919: In January, Hemingway returns from Italy to Oak Park, where in March he receives a letter from Agnes Von Kurowsky saying that she will not marry him. In May, Ernest retreats to Walloon Lake and Petoskey, Michigan, where he remains through the fall and early winter, returning to Oak Park in time for Christmas. During this period he writes short stories modeled on those in *The Saturday Evening Post* magazine, none of which are accepted for publication. They include the stories now known as "The Woppian Way," "The Mercenaries," and "The Current."

1920: In January, Hemingway departs from Chicago for Toronto, Canada, to take a job as tutor to a young boy. While there he begins writing freelance feature stories for *The Toronto Star*. In May he returns briefly to Oak Park and then to Walloon Lake, where, shortly after his twenty-first birthday, his mother evicts him from their cottage for his irritating behavior. In October, Ernest moves into a shared apartment in Chicago, where he meets his wife-to-be, Hadley Richardson, from St. Louis. That December he takes a job editing a short-lived trade publication, the *Cooperative Commonwealth*. During this period he continues writing short stories, such as "The Ash-Heels Tendon," all of which go unpublished, and he courts Hadley with almost daily letters.

1921: In March, Hemingway visits Hadley in St. Louis, where their engagement is made public. He is twenty-two; she is thirty. That summer he remains in Chicago working and writing short fiction, including the first version of "Up in Michigan," which will become his first mature story. In September, Ernest and Hadley are married at Horton Bay, Michigan, and honeymoon in the Walloon Lake cottage. That fall, corrupt management of the *Cooperative Commonwealth* creates a scandal that leads to the closing of the venture, and Hemingway, who wants to return to Italy, is advised by Sherwood Anderson that Paris is the place for a young writer. In December, Ernest and Hadley sail from New York bound for France.

1922: In January the Hemingways move into a second-floor walk-up on the Left Bank in Paris. In February and March, Ernest meets Sylvia Beach, Ezra Pound, and Gertrude Stein. In November, Hemingway is in Lausanne, Switzerland, reporting for *The Toronto Star* on the Lausanne Peace Conference, convened to settle Greece and Turkey's territorial disputes. In December, Hadley, in tears, joins him there, reporting that all of his stories were stolen when a train thief made off with her valise.

1923: By January, Hadley is pregnant. With William Bird and Robert McAlmon, Hemingway makes his first trip to Spain in June. He and Hadley return in July to attend their first San Fermín festival in Pamplona. In August *Three Stories & Ten Poems* is published in Paris by McAlmon's Contact Press; in August the Hemingways return to Toronto, where their son, John (called "Bumby"), is born on 10 October.

1924: In January, having quit his job with the *Star,* Ernest takes Hadley and son back to Paris, where they move into a Left Bank apartment. In mid March, Hemingway's collection of vignettes is published in Paris as *in our time* by William Bird's Three Mountains Press. From February through April, Ernest works as an unpaid assistant to Ford Madox Ford editing the *transatlantic review.* During this period most of the stories to appear in *In Our Time* (1925) are written. "Indian Camp" is published in the *transatlantic.* In May, Ernest begins writing "Big Two-Hearted River." That summer the Hemingways and friends are back in Spain for their second San Fermín festival. At the end of September the typescript for *In Our Time* is sent to New York. The *transatlantic review* publishes Hemingway's "The Doctor and the Doctor's Wife" in the November issue and "Cross-Country Snow" in the December issue.

1925: In March, Hemingway accepts Boni and Liveright's offer to publish *In Our Time.* In April, Hemingway meets F. Scott Fitzgerald in Paris. The May issue of *This Quarter* publishes "Big Two-Hearted River." That summer the Hemingways and friends are back in Spain for the Pamplona festival. Immediately following San Fermín, Ernest begins writing *The Sun Also Rises,* finishing the first draft in Paris in September. On 5 October, *In Our Time* is published in New York. In November, Hemingway begins *The Torrents of Spring,* which he will use to break his contract with Boni and Liveright. At the end of the year Horace Liveright rejects *The Torrents of Spring,* which satirizes his prominent author, Sherwood Anderson.

1926: In January, Ernest goes to New York to negotiate a new publishing contract. On his stopover in Paris, his affair with Pauline Pfeiffer begins. In February, Hemingway officially leaves Liveright and signs a contract with Charles Scribner's Sons publishing house, beginning his twenty-one-year relationship with his new editor, Maxwell Perkins. In April, back in Paris, Ernest sends *The Sun Also Rises* to Scribners. On 28 May, Scribners publishes *Torrents of Spring* as part of their contract with Hemingway. In June, Fitzgerald critiques *The Sun Also Rises*, advising a substantial cutting of the opening chapter. In July the Hemingways return to Pamplona with Pauline Pfeiffer and Gerald and Sara Murphy. In August, Ernest and Hadley return to Paris to set up separate residences, their marriage finished; later that month Hemingway returns corrected galleys for *The Sun Also Rises*. On 22 October *The Sun Also Rises* is published in New York. In December, Ernest files for divorce in Paris. During the previous three months he has written "A Canary for One," "The Killers," "In Another Country," and "Now I Lay Me."

1927: In March the *Atlantic Monthly* accepts Hemingway's story "Fifty Grand" for publication. In April, Hadley and Ernest are divorced. In May he and Pauline marry in Paris and honeymoon at Le Grau-du-Roi in Provence. Later that month he completes "Ten Indians" and "Hills Like White Elephants." In July the Hemingways return to Pamplona for the San Fermín feria (festival). On 14 October, Scribners publishes Hemingway's second collection of short stories, *Men Without Women*.

1928: By February, Pauline is pregnant. In March, Hemingway begins writing *A Farewell to Arms*. That same month the Hemingways sail for Key West, Florida. On 28 June his second son, Patrick, is born by cesarean section in Kansas City. In August, Hemingway completes the first draft of *A Farewell to Arms*. On 6 December his father, Clarence Hemingway, commits suicide in Oak Park.

1929: In January the typescript of *A Farewell to Arms* is prepared, which Perkins picks up in Key West in February. *Scribner's Magazine* offers $16,000 for the serialization of the novel prior to publication. In April, Ernest, Pauline, John, and Patrick depart from Havana for France, where they return to their Paris apartment. On 27 September *A Farewell to Arms* is published in New York.

1930: In January the Hemingways depart from Paris to take up residence in Key West. In mid March, Hemingway begins his treatise on the bullfight—*Death in the Afternoon*. In July, Ernest, Pauline, and both sons travel to the L-Bar-T Ranch on the Wyoming edge of Yellowstone Park, where they remain all summer and into the fall.

1931: In January the Hemingways return to Key West, where they buy a house on Whitehead Street at the end of April. By this time Pauline is two months pregnant with her second child. Ernest's third son, Gregory, is delivered by cesarean section in Kansas City on 12 November.

1932: In January, Hemingway finishes the first draft of *Death in the Afternoon.* In March he writes "After the Storm." In August, while he and Pauline are at the L-Bar-T Ranch, Ernest writes "The Light of the World." On 23 September *Death in the Afternoon* is published in New York. Back in Key West, Ernest writes "Fathers and Sons" in November. The Hemingways are in Pauline's hometown, Piggott, Arkansas, from Thanksgiving through Christmas. Here Hemingway finishes "A Clean, Well-Lighted Place."

1933: In January, Hemingway is in New York on business and meets Thomas Wolfe and Arnold Gingrich, editor of the newly founded magazine *Esquire.* Hemingway returns to Key West, where he finishes four short stories between February and April. While in Havana in July he writes "Marlin Off the Morro," his first essay for *Esquire,* and completes the stories that will appear in *Winner Take Nothing.* In August the Hemingways sail from Havana for Europe. *Winner Take Nothing* is published in New York on 27 October. In Paris, Hemingway finishes "One Trip Across," the Harry Morgan story that will become part of *To Have and Have Not.* In December, Ernest and Pauline embark on a two-month safari in what is then British East Africa.

1934: In February the Hemingways leave Africa and return to Paris. In April the family is back in Key West, where Ernest soon begins his nonfiction book *Green Hills of Africa,* based on his recent safari experience. In November he finishes the first draft of *Green Hills of Africa.*

1935: In May, *Scribner's Magazine* publishes the first serial installment of *Green Hills of Africa.* The book version of *Green Hills of Africa* is published on 25 October. In November and December the Hemingways remain in Key West, where Ernest is writing the second Harry Morgan story, "The Tradesman's Return."

1936: In April, Hemingway finishes drafts of "The Short Happy Life of Francis Macomber" and "The Snows of Kilimanjaro." From August to October he and Pauline are at the L-Bar-T ranch, where Ernest works on his Harry Morgan novel, *To Have and Have Not.* At Thanksgiving the North American News Alliance (NANA) hires Hemingway as a journalist to report on the Spanish Civil War. Through December, Ernest works to bring the Morgan novel to completion. That same month he meets Martha Gellhorn in Key West.

1937: Hemingway leaves for Europe in February. In March he is in Madrid, where he is joined by Martha Gellhorn. Throughout April he writes news stories for NANA and works with the director Joris Ivens on his documentary *The Spanish Earth,* for which Hemingway writes the narration. In May he sails from France for New York. In June he completes work on *The Spanish Earth* and gives Scribners his finished novel, *To Have and Have Not.* Hemingway returns to the Spanish war in August. *To Have and Have Not* is published on 15 October, by which time Martha and Ernest are in Madrid, where he is writing his play, *The Fifth Column,* and working for NANA.

1938: At the end of January, Ernest and Pauline return to Key West, their marriage coming apart. In March, Ernest returns to France, meeting Martha in Paris. In May he returns alone to New York and Key West. On 22 October *The Fifth Column and the First Forty-Nine Stories* is published in New York. At the end of November, Pauline meets Ernest in New York, and they return to Key West.

1939: In January *The Fifth Column* is in production in New York. In February, Hemingway moves into the Ambos Mundos Hotel in Havana to begin writing *For Whom the Bell Tolls.* In May, Martha rents La Finca Vigía, a run-down country place outside of Havana. Ernest moves in with her. In late August he and all three of his sons are at the L-Bar-T ranch, where Pauline joins them. With their marriage in ruins, Ernest sends Pauline and the children back to Key West and invites Martha to join him in the West. In November, Martha sails

Michigan, summer of 1913. "The smell of pine smoke and the odor of fresh coffee could bring it all back to him no matter how far distant. Another summer in another country, with only his map and its blue markings to remind him, he would write of *Big Two-Hearted River,* fishing with his mind that water which he had married young." (Michael Reynolds, *The Young Hemingway,* 1986)

from New York to report on the war in Finland. A month later Ernest returns to Key West, where he takes the ferry to Havana, his marriage to Pauline finished.

1940: For the first seven months of the year, Hemingway remains in Cuba, living with Martha in Finca Vigía and working on *For Whom the Bell Tolls*. On 7 March, *The Fifth Column* opens in New York to mixed reviews. At the end of July, Hemingway delivers to Scribners the finished draft of *For Whom the Bell Tolls,* which is published on 21 October to rave reviews. In November, Hemingway's divorce from Pauline becomes final; later that month he and Martha are married in Cheyenne, Wyoming. Back in Cuba in December, Ernest buys the Finca Vigía.

1941: At the end of January, Ernest and Martha set out as journalists to the China-Japan war zone. Between February and April, they are in Hawaii, Hong Kong, Namyung, Canton, Chungking, and Rangoon.

1942: Between March and August, Hemingway edits and writes a preface for a collection called *Men at War, The Best War Stories of All Time,* which is published by Crown on 22 October. In May, German submarines begin a systematic attack on American oil tankers in the Caribbean and the Gulf of Mexico. At the request of the American ambassador to Cuba, Hemingway creates a network of informants gathering intelligence on Spanish Falangists and German nationals living in Cuba. At the same time, he proposes using his fishing boat, the *Pilar,* for armed patrols in Cuban waters. From late July to mid November, the *Pilar* makes short patrols along the northwest coast of Cuba.

1943: From January to March, Hemingway continues with short antisubmarine patrols. In September, Martha leaves for England to report on the war for *Collier's* magazine. Hemingway refuses to join her as a journalist, their marriage having become a series of arguments and accusations. Alone at the Finca, he is morose, lonely, and drinking too much.

1944: In February, Hemingway closes down the *Pilar* patrols and agrees to be a journalist for *Collier's*. In May he flies to England, soon meeting Mary Welsh. Later that month Martha arrives in London. She and Ernest have angry words. At the same time his affair with Mary is an open secret among the correspondents. On 6 June, Hemingway is aboard a landing craft taking soldiers ashore at the Fox Green sector of Omaha Beach. He returns to the troopship with the landing craft to write "Voyage to Victory," which appears in *Collier's* on 22 July. In

June, Hemingway flies missions with the British RAF. In July he is assigned to General George Patton's command as a frontline journalist. Later that month he transfers himself to the 22nd Infantry Regiment. In August, Hemingway commands French Resistance fighters at Rambouillet, outside Paris. On 25 August, with the liberating French and American armies, he enters Paris and moves into the Ritz Hotel, where Mary Welsh, herself a correspondent, soon joins him.

1945: In March, with the European war winding down, Hemingway departs from Paris to return to Cuba, where he is joined by Mary Welsh in May. Martha Gellhorn agrees to a divorce on grounds that she deserted Ernest, but he does not start proceedings until September. In October he begins work on a novel that is set in Bimini and will eventually become *Islands in the Stream*. In November he sells the movie rights to "The Killers" and "The Short Happy Life of Francis Macomber." In December his divorce from Martha becomes final.

1946: In the first half of the year, Hemingway sinks into one of his recurring depressed periods, although he writes steadily on the Bimini novel, completing one thousand pages of manuscript by July. In June he and Mary are married in Havana.

1947: From January through March, Hemingway remains in Cuba working on the Bimini novel. On 13 June, Hemingway is awarded a Bronze Star for his several activities during World War II. During August and September he is peripherally involved in an aborted attempt to overthrow the dictator of the Dominican Republic. He leaves Cuba just ahead of a government inquiry.

1948: After returning to Cuba early in the year, the Hemingways sail in September from Havana to Italy, where they revisit Ernest's World War I sites and experience Venice for the first time. From there they move to an isolated hotel on the almost deserted island of Torcello, where Ernest writes "On the Blue Water" for *Holiday* magazine. In mid December the Hemingways move into a rented house in the mountain ski resort of Cortina, Italy. By this time Ernest has met a nineteen-year-old Italian girl, Adriana Ivancich, with whom he falls in unrequited love.

1949: In early March the Hemingways return briefly to Venice, where they meet Sinclair Lewis. Back at Cortina, Ernest begins a short story about a duck hunt on the Venetian marshes that will grow into the novel *Across the River and into the Trees*. At the end of April the Hemingways sail from Genoa to return to Cuba. All that summer and into the fall, Hemingway works on the Venetian novel. In September he contracts with *Cosmopolitan* to serialize the book.

1950: In February the first installment of *Across the River and into the Trees* runs in *Cosmopolitan*. On 13 May, Lillian Ross's profile of Hemingway appears in *The New Yorker*. On 7 September the book version of *Across the River and into the Trees* is published in New York. In October, Adriana and her mother Dora Ivancich arrive at the Finca by Hemingway's invitation. During November and December, while the Ivancichs are in residence, Ernest completes his Bimini novel, calling it "The Island and the Stream."

1951: Early in January, Hemingway begins what he calls the fourth section of the Bimini book, but it becomes *The Old Man and the Sea*. In March *Holiday* prints two short Hemingway fables, "The Faithful Bull" and "The Good Lion," both illustrated by Adriana. In April *True* magazine prints his nonfiction story of an antelope hunt called "The Shot." From April through October, Hemingway makes extensive revisions and additions to his Bimini novel. On 28 July, Hemingway's mother, Grace, dies in Memphis, Tennessee. He does not go to the funeral.

1952: In a five-million-copy single issue of *Life* magazine, *The Old Man and the Sea* is published on 1 September. The novel is simultaneously released in hardcover by Scribners and is the Book-of-the-Month Club's featured selection. It becomes an immediate best-seller.

1953: On 4 May, Hemingway is awarded the Pulitzer Prize. In June the Hemingways sail from New York, bound for Europe and Africa. In July they leave Paris by car for Spain, where Ernest has not been since 1939. He takes Mary to her first feria of San Fermín in Pamplona; he has not attended the spectacle since 1931. In September, Ernest and Mary begin a four-month safari in Africa.

1954: On 21 July, Hemingway's fifty-fifth birthday, he is awarded the Order of Carlos Manuel de Céspedes by the Cuban government. On 28 October he is told that he has received the Nobel Prize in literature, but he pleads ill health as a reason not to attend the ceremony. At the Finca he has begun writing a semifictional account of his safari, which is published posthumously in 1999 as *True at First Light*.

1955: Between January and June, Hemingway writes steadily on his "fictional memoir" of the safari and stops work on it between July and

September to assist with the filming of *The Old Man and the Sea.* He returns to the book in October and November.

1956: In February, Hemingway is once again assisting with the filming of *The Old Man and the Sea,* which stars Spencer Tracy. In May the Hemingways return to La Finca Vigía, where Ernest writes several short stories about World War II. In September the Hemingways return to Europe. In Paris, Ernest discovers his typescripts and notebooks from the 1920s left stored in the Ritz Hotel.

1957: In January the Hemingways return to New York. Returning to the Finca, Ernest begins writing a complicated story set on the Provence coast, a novel that will grow into the posthumously published *The Garden of Eden* (1986). In July, with the Provence novel in progress and the African novel unfinished, Hemingway begins writing a somewhat fictionalized version of his early memories of Paris, published posthumously in 1964 as *A Moveable Feast.* From October through December, Ernest is at the Finca alternating between work on his African novel and his memoir.

1958: Between January and July, Hemingway writes steadily on his Paris memoir and *The Garden of Eden.* The April issue of *The Paris Review* features George Plimpton's detailed interview with Hemingway on the art of his fiction. As the Castro revolution in Cuba gains momentum, Ernest and Mary begin looking for a safe haven until the results are clear. In August they rent a house in Ketchum, Idaho, for the winter. By the end of the year Hemingway has completed most of his Paris memoir.

1959: In January and February, Hemingway works steadily on *The Garden of Eden.* In April the Hemingways buy the Dan Topping house in Ketchum. In April they board ship for Spain. In May, Ernest writes "The Art of the Short Story" before the corrida (bullfighting) season begins. From June through September he follows the *mano-a-mano* (competitive) bullfights of Antonio Ordóñez and Luis Miguel Dominguín. Throughout the summer his erratic behavior puts an added strain on his marriage. In September, Mary flies back to Havana, threatening to leave Ernest. In October, Hemingway sails from Spain for New York, where he delivers a copy of his Paris memoir to Scribners. The year ends with Ernest becoming more and more withdrawn and paranoid.

1960: From January through May, Hemingway writes his account of the Ordóñez-Dominguín corridas, a portion of which will be published in *Life;* an edited version is published posthumously as *The Danger-*

ous Summer (1985). In August, Hemingway flies to Spain to collect more information for his corrida book. In Spain, Ernest's mental condition grows steadily worse. He returns to New York in October, after which he and Mary return to their house in Ketchum. That fall his erratic moods, paranoia, and despondency become worse. On 30 November, Ernest is flown to the Mayo Clinic in Minnesota, where he undergoes electroshock treatments.

1961: On 22 January, Hemingway is released from the Mayo Clinic and returns to Ketchum. For the next two months he remains withdrawn, loses considerable weight, and becomes more morose, feeling that he cannot write. He is unable to bring his Paris memoir to closure, and he worries excessively about libel suits. On 21 April, after attempting suicide, Hemingway is sedated and hospitalized in Ketchum. Three days later, a second attempt to kill himself is thwarted. The next day he is flown back to the Mayo Clinic for more electroshock therapy. The doctors release him on 26 June, and he and Mary return to the Ketchum house. At 7:30 A.M. on 2 July, Hemingway uses his favorite shotgun to take his own life.

ABOUT ERNEST HEMINGWAY

Born: 21 July 1899 in Oak Park, Illinois

Died: 2 July 1961 in Ketchum, Idaho

Married: Hadley Richardson, 3 September 1921 (divorced 14 April 1927);
married Pauline Pfeiffer, 10 May 1927 (divorced 4 November 1940);
married Martha Gellhorn, 21 November 1940 (divorced 21 December
1945); married Mary Welsh, 14 March 1946.

Education: Oak Park and River Forest High School

Ernest Hemingway was born on 21 July 1899 in Oak Park, Illinois, an early and affluent suburb of Chicago. His father, Clarence Edmonds Hemingway, who graduated from Oberlin College and Rush Medical College, was a respected professional whose specialty became obstetrics. Dr. Hemingway was an avid outdoorsman, hunter, fisherman, and naturalist. In Oak Park he founded a local Agassiz Club, introducing boys to natural history. Hemingway's mother, Grace Hall Hemingway, was a well-trained contralto who had at least two New York City performances before marrying Dr. Hemingway. In Oak Park, she enjoyed a lengthy career as a voice and music teacher, choir director, and, later in life, as a largely self-taught painter. Young Hemingway grew up with an older sister, Marcelline, and three younger sisters, Ursula, Madelaine, and Carol. He had one younger brother, Leicester. Both of his grandfathers served in the Grand Army of the Republic during the Civil War, and young Ernest heard war stories at the knee of Grandfather Anson Hemingway, a real-estate developer. While Ernest was growing up, he saw horses disappear from the village streets to be replaced by automobiles. His was the first generation to grow up with consumer technology that was both liberating and alienating, creating an enormous gap between nineteenth-century parents and twentieth-century children.

Milan, Italy, fall of 1918. Ernest Hemingway poses in his newly tailored military uniform, which, with its U.S. insignia, bears no resemblance to the Red Cross uniform he should be wearing. On 8 July 1918, thirteen days shy of his nineteenth birthday, he was wounded when an Austrian trench-mortar shell landed directly on the forward observation post where he was trying to get a close look at the enemy across the Piava River.

In the Oak Park of his youth, Hemingway was theoretically protected by city ordinances from uncensored movies, boxing matches, any information on venereal disease or birth control, all forms of gambling and prostitution, and all consumption of alcohol. Should there have been an illegitimate birth within the village, neither parent's name could appear on the birth certificate without his or her consent. Until he turned eighteen, Hemingway could not legally buy cigarettes, play billiards, or drive a car within the village limits. Unless accompanied by a parent or responsible adult, young Hemingway, governed by the village curfew, could not be out of the house after 8:00 P.M. in the fall and winter, or after 9:00 P.M. in the spring and summer.[1] On a sweltering July day, an Oak Parker could not buy a beer within the village limits. But uncensored movies and cold beer were only a nickel trolley ride away. Or if a boy could not spare the nickel, he could walk across the avenue into Cicero, where all manner of forbidden activity was possible. But not in Oak Park. Not yet. At least not in public.

By the time Hemingway was in grade school, Oak Park, established as a haven from which to escape the threat of Chicago fires and Chicago vice, was no longer isolated from big-city temptations. Five different trolley lines connected husbands to their downtown jobs, wives to Marshall Field's department store and the Chicago Art Institute, and teenage boys to whatever teenage boys found most alluring. The cows that once grazed in the vacant Oak Park lots had mostly disappeared along with the lots, which were now filling up with houses. The Censorship Committee worked overtime to keep the youth of Oak Park innocent, but of course it was an impossible task. Their stringent movie code kept the most pernicious Hollywood influence just outside the village limits, but those boundaries were becoming less and less effective.

No matter how conservative their politics might be, Oak Parkers were always progressive. Their streets were paved and lighted when parts of Chicago were still muddy; their water system was the most sanitary possible; the hospital, the library, and the high school were all of premier quality. At Oak Park and River Forest High School, Hemingway took the then-standard precollege curriculum: six semesters of science, four of math, six of Latin, eight of English literature and composition, four of history, two of applied music, and two years of orchestra. In Latin, young Hemingway translated his Cicero; in history he wrote essays on Greek tyrants and the Marathon campaign, and outlined the Punic Wars. His yearlong courses in American and ancient history were not grounded in watered-down student texts: Hemingway's generation read and were tested on the standard histories of their day. In English courses, all of which required weekly writing and the study of composition, young Hemingway read the classic myths, Geoffrey Chaucer, Edmund Spenser, William Shakespeare, John Milton, Alexander Pope, the British Romantics, Sir Walter Scott, Charles Dickens, George Eliot, Alfred Tennyson, Robert Browning, and Matthew Arnold. He spent ten weeks studying the history of the English language, four weeks on formal rhetoric, and an entire semester of his senior year on prose composition.[2] Along with his classmates, Hemingway memorized the opening lines of Chaucer's "General Prologue" to *The Canterbury Tales* and the then-standard ration of Shakespeare's soliloquies.[3] Whatever the course, humanities or science, there were always written assignments: weekly book reports, essays, and term papers. Hemingway outlined his reading of *Macbeth* and *Hamlet* and wrote reports on the anatomy of grasshoppers, the necessity of life insurance, the need for a standing army, and the causes of the American Revolution.[4]

In 1918, with America now dedicated to helping England, France, and Italy defeat the German and Austro-Hungarian forces mounted against them in World War I, Hemingway tried to enlist in the army, but was rejected for poor eyesight. That spring, he volunteered to drive Red Cross ambulances on the Italian front, where, on 8 July 1918, he was seriously wounded. In 1919 he came back changed by his war experience to find the cultural bulwarks of Oak Park firmly in place—the First Congregational Church (now First United), the Scoville Institute (public library), the Oak Park and River Forest High School, and the Nineteenth Century Club. These were the shaping community forces, providing Hemingway's generation with a sense of identity and strong behavioral models. Between the turn of the century and the end of World War I, Oak Park worked hard at the moral and cultural education of its young. Above all, it taught its sons that, whatever the game, winning was important. The "Strenuous Life" advocated by Theodore Roosevelt was the village code and the high-school athlete's model. Wherever one listened in Oak Park—church, civic clubs, or the newspaper—he was told that physical, mental, and moral condition correlated: better body, better grades, better boy. Young Hemingway, who was never much of an athlete, became a lifelong, fierce competitor. Twice he ran the high-school cross-country race. Twice he finished last. But he finished. Whatever he did in life—fishing, hiking, hunting, writing, loving, learning—it was a competitive venture, a challenge match to be won or lost. Many of his fictional characters behave this way as well. The competitive trait runs deep in the American vein, a trait that Hemingway learned there in the heart of the country.

Along with the competitive spirit, Hemingway also learned early the necessity for hard work. Work was not something he always enjoyed. Indeed, he sometimes railed against it. But to be a man in America one was expected to work hard, always, and Hemingway held himself to that rigorous ethic for most of his life. When he was not working hard, he felt guilty; when he felt most guilty, he turned his pleasures into work. In 1933, in the heart of the Great Depression, when a quarter of the work force had no work, Hemingway spent $25,000 on his first African safari. (In today's dollars that would be at least $150,000.) Conspicuous consumption surely, but it was not only for his pleasure. He wrote several colorful *Esquire* articles during the course of the hunt, and afterward wrote *Green Hills of Africa* (1935). For most, that safari would have been only a vacation; Hemingway, steeped as he was in the work ethic, made it a working vacation. Later, he spent a good deal of time on the Gulf Stream fishing, but it was not merely for fun; he was relentlessly researching the marlin for a book of natural history he never got around to writing. Instead he created *The Old Man and the Sea* (1952).

"For a true writer each book should be a new beginning where he tries again for something that is beyond attainment. He should always try for something that has never been done or that others have tried and failed. Then sometimes, with great luck, he will succeed."

Ernest Hemingway

From Hemingway's Nobel Prize acceptance speech, read for him by John C. Cabot, U.S. ambassador to Sweden, on 10 December 1954.

One of the lessons Hemingway learned early and late was that money mattered in Oak Park and the world, an easy lesson to absorb, for it was not small change that cultivated those wide lawns or paid for the Frank Lloyd Wright–designed houses. The Hemingway family, while respected, was never wealthy, but Ernest saw the spoils of wealth wherever he looked. If he left the village with an empty pocket in 1919, he never intended to remain in that condition. Other experimental writers were content to publish in small literary magazines that paid little if anything for their fiction. Hemingway began like that as he learned his trade, but his sights were always set much higher. With the exception of his journalism, Hemingway never wrote merely for money, but he always expected top dollar for what he wrote and never sold himself short. That too he learned in Oak Park.

With its insistence on winning and its disdain for anything less than the best, Oak Park put a good deal of pressure on its sons and daughters. That some, like Hemingway, seemed to rebel against those pressures is not surprising. That later readers have taken that rebellion as

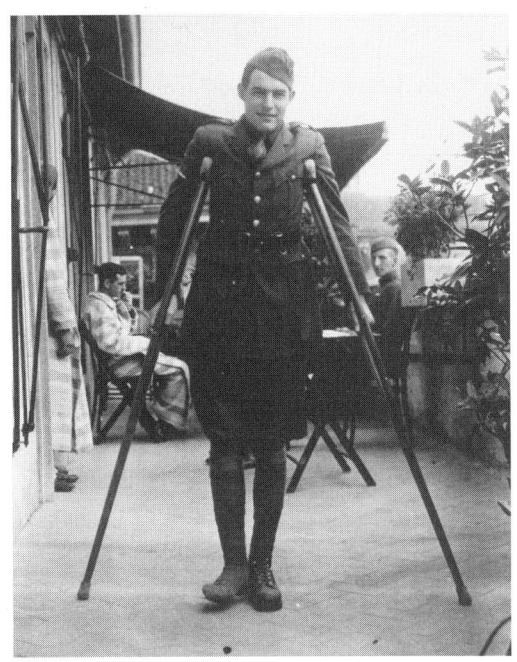

Milan, Italy, 1918. On the balcony of the American Red Cross Hospital where he is recovering from surgery on his damaged right knee. Although Hemingway exaggerated his war record, for the rest of his life he will feel that he is different from those who have never been seriously wounded.

Hemingway's rejection of Oak Park is unfortunate, for nothing could be further from the truth. One cannot reject his cultural inheritance any more than he can reject his blood type. Ernest may have left Oak Park in 1919, but he carried a piece of the village with him always. After his Paris years in the 1920s, he bought and maintained Oak Parkish homes, first in Key West and then in Cuba—large, lawned homes with swimming pools, gardens and gardeners, cooks, and maids— homes that marked the presence of a personage.

Hemingway grew up with sisters, a live-in nursemaid, and a talented mother. Grace Hall Hemingway was a public performer who was usually the center of attention, whether she was conducting the church choir, instructing voice students, singing in her well-trained contralto voice, or, later, selling her paintings. She dominated the home in which Ernest grew up. Most boys rebel against their fathers; Hemingway had no choice but to rebel against his mother. She was a strong, talented woman, five of whose six children became artists in various fields: one a ceramicist, one a musician, one a playwright and public lecturer, and two writers. Some mothers lived for their children, basking in their deeds, but not Hemingway's mother. Never behaving like the mothers of his friends, she was always doing something different, dressing differently, or marching for the vote. Sometimes in Oak Park his performing mother was an embarrassment to him; sometimes her impossible way of professing joy in the least likely circumstances was enough to anger anyone. She was a big woman with a big voice who never doubted her own worth. In the summer of 1920, after a series of infuriating conflicts with her son, Grace Hemingway threw Ernest out of their summer cottage on Walloon Lake, Michigan, calling him a menace to youth and telling him to grow up.

While Ernest learned about counterpoint, melody, and tempo from his mother, it was his father, Clarence Hemingway, who took him to the woods where his deep passions were rooted. Ernest responded to all of his father's interests: hiking, hunting, fishing, and natural history. Every summer between 1900 and 1918, Hemingway spent at least two months at the Walloon Lake family cottage located close to Petoskey, Michigan, on the lower peninsula. There Ernest found a freedom he seldom knew in Oak Park, freedom to roam the lake and woods, to fish for trout, and to observe the last of the Ojibway Indians living in the area. It was as close to a frontier experience as was possible in that era. Hemingway's earliest mature fiction, written in 1924 in Paris, would use the lake setting, and even later in life he would return to Walloon for the setting of his posthumously published stories "The Summer People" and "The Last Good Country." The Agassiz Club nature outings in the spring, summers on Walloon Lake, fall bird hunts, and winter visits to the Field Museum of Natural History in Chicago all were formative elements in young Hemingway's education, shaping his interests to the end of his life.

By the time Hemingway was twelve years old, his father grew more and more distant from the older son who worshiped him. As early as 1904, the doctor began suffering from spells that his family called "nervousness" and today is called depression. Periodically, Clarence Hemingway took rest cures, but his depression, paranoia, and emotional isolation grew gradually worse. Neither Ernest nor his siblings understood their father's erratic moods, which made him less and less accessible to them. In 1928, at the age of fifty-seven, suffering from depression, paranoia, angina, and diabetes, Clarence Hemingway lay down on his marriage bed and put a bullet through his head. Ernest, perhaps not wanting to admit to his father's physical and mental problems, blamed his mother, saying she drove his father to kill himself. But by the time he was sixty-one, Ernest was suffering from his father's syndrome, made worse by physical injuries and alcohol.

After he was eighteen Hemingway never lived again in the village of Oak Park, but many of his characters, beneath their hard exteriors, are not without Oak Park virtues. His men may drink and curse in a way calculated to offend women like his mother, but beneath that surface they are men who mourn the loss of values. In *A Farewell to Arms* (1929), words like *nobility, loyalty,* and *honor* may have become obscene to Frederic Henry, but only the words, not the values themselves. They never lost their currency. Add love. Add courage. Add hard work and self-reliance. And above all else, add duty. In *Islands in the Stream* (1970) Thomas Hudson, talking to himself, says, "Love you lose. Honor has been gone a long time. Duty you do." Most of Hemingway's major characters make their pilgrimage graveward accompanied by those good friends. They sustain Robert Jordan at the hour of his death in *For Whom the Bell Tolls*

"Chief among Hemingway's virtues as a writer is his scrupulous regard for fact, for reality, for 'what happened.' It is a rare virtue in the world of letters. Most writers want to please or shock, to be 'accomplished craftsmen' or to be 'original'; in both cases their work is determined by literary fashions, which they either follow or defy. From the very first, Hemingway did neither, since his aim was simply to reproduce the things he had seen and felt–'simply,' I say, but anyone who has tried to set down his own impressions accurately must realize that the task is enormously difficult; there is always the temptation to change and falsify the story because it doesn't fit into a conventional pattern, or because the right words are lacking."

Malcolm Cowley

From "Hemingway: Work in Progress," *The New Republic* (20 October 1937): 305-306.

(1940). Colonel Cantwell in *Across the River and Into the Trees* (1950) and Thomas Hudson, in their last good nights, never forget them. And where one finds them most lacking, in *The Sun Also Rises* (1926), life is stale, flat, and profitless.

It was the world that had changed, not Hemingway's values. Like many Oak Parkers, he, too, was filled with loathing for a world that no longer honored the old verities. The boy, who was weaned on the maxims and example of Theodore Roosevelt, grew up to find Teddy reduced to a caricature by the Jazz Age. Like so many modernist writers, Hemingway remembered all his life the lost world in which he grew up, the early world of Oak Park, its people and its culture. His characters, going down to loneliness or death in other countries, might have no home or family, but between and beneath the lines, many of them are good Oak Parkers, and their creator, for all his surface dissimilarities to the people of his hometown, was and remained a boy from the village.

Hemingway's storytelling frequently involves an experienced character passing along information, advice, or rules of behavior to a less experienced character: teacher and tyro. In and out of fiction, Hemingway was always teaching someone how to box, fish, hunt, or write; how to travel; how to get full return for money spent; where to stay and what to do there. In Oak Park, he was giving boxing lessons to his friends; at Walloon he taught young visitors how to catch trout. Early in Paris, he claimed that he was trading Ezra Pound boxing lessons for writing lessons. This instructional intensity runs throughout Hemingway's writing life. *The Sun Also Rises* may be the "hell of a sad story" that Ernest said it was, but it is also a marvelous guide to the Left Bank of Paris in the 1920s, and an equally accurate guide to the *feria* (festival) of San Fermín. Read *The Sun Also Rises* to learn which train to catch, where to get off, the view from the bus, and where to stay in Pamplona. By the end of the novel, Hemingway has provided an insider's knowledge about the food, the wine, the music, and the kinds of permissible behavior. The reader knows the daily routine of the *feria*, starting with the morning *encierro* (running of the bulls) and ending with the evening fireworks. He has learned about the *corrida* (bullfight), its three-part structure, and the artistry of a skilled matador.

As a natural historian, Hemingway not only described the fish, the bird, or the animal so clearly that it was real, but he also gave clinical details on its behavior and its capture. To catch river trout using grasshoppers on a fly line, read "Big Two-Hearted River," where Hemingway teaches not only how to bait the hook but how to make camp in the good place. Before going marlin fishing, read Hemingway's several essays on the subject to learn every step from fixing the baits to boating the fish. It was not enough for Hemingway to write an interesting story. He wanted the reader to be instructed as well as involved in the narrative. Turn to the appendices of *Death in the Afternoon* (1932) for an eighty-three-page glossary "of certain words, terms and phrases used in bullfighting." Read further in any of his books or essays to discover his interests in military tactics, politics, literary history, landscape painting, and topography, interests that give his characters and narrators a professional edge that makes their story convincing.

One does not have to read far in Hemingway to find the high physical and emotional costs of bodily wounds. He learned the lesson early, late, and frequently during his tumultuous life. On the night of 8 July 1918, he was wounded by an Austrian trench-mortar shell while standing in an Italian forward observation post at Fossalta on the Piave River. The two Italians standing next to him both died. Hemingway woke up to a ruined right knee, a first-class concussion, and legs full of small shrapnel; a machine-gun bullet hit his foot while he was being carried back to the aid station. In the fall of 1930, while on a Wyoming bear hunt, the right side of Hemingway's face was laid open when his horse bolted through the woods. A night trip to a veterinarian got the cut closed with stitches, leaving an interesting scar. Two months later, outside of Billings, Montana, the car that Ernest was driving turned over in a ditch, leaving him with a compound spiral fracture of his writing arm between elbow and shoulder. It was five months before the nerves in his right hand began to work again. While on safari in 1933–1934, he contracted a severe case of amebic dysentery, requiring emergency treatment. During a London blackout in 1944, he was in an auto accident that badly gashed his scalp and gave him another serious concussion, which was renewed two months later in France when his jeep was overturned by German tank fire. Ten years later, Hemingway survived two African plane crashes while suffering numerous internal and external injuries, including another serious concussion.

Walloon Lake, northern Michigan, summer of 1919. Friends who became characters in Hemingway's fiction. Left to right: Carl Edgar, Katy Smith, Marcelline Hemingway, Bill Horne, Ernest with his pistol, and Bill Smith. Katy later married the writer and Hemingway friend John Dos Passos. Hemingway, here the youngest of the group, remembered his summer life on the lake as one of those "last good places."

Given these traumatic experiences and remembering that he was a doctor's son, it is not surprising to find wounded men proliferating in Hemingway's fiction. The Indian father in "Indian Camp" lies in his upper bunk, his leg wounded by his axe. In the vignettes published as *in our time* (1924), Nick Adams lies wounded against the wall. In later stories Nick is shell-shocked ("A Way You'll Never Be") and unable to sleep ("Now I Lay Me"). Frederic Henry in *A Farewell to Arms* is blown up much as Hemingway was during World War I. In *The Sun Also Rises*, Jake Barnes has suffered a sexually maiming wound while flying on the Italian front. Wherever one looks, the wounded pile up: bullfighters gored and bleeding; Harry Morgan dying slowly from being gut shot by a Cuban revolutionist in *To Have and Have Not* (1937); Robert Jordan's leg ruined by a shell explosion in *For Whom the Bell Tolls*; Thomas Hudson dying from gunshot wounds at the end of *Islands in the Stream*. The incursion of random violence into the lives of his characters reflected not only Hemingway's own experiences but also his observation of twentieth-century life, where gratuitous violence became, during his lifetime, a frightening norm.

Hemingway's firsthand observation of violence was considerable. During the Normandy invasion on 6 June 1944 he rode into the Fox Green sector of Omaha Beach in a landing craft delivering troops to an already bloody battleground, and returned to his ship to write about the accuracy of the German gunfire. Out of his multiple experiences came four war novels and several short stories, all of which remind the reader that the twentieth century will probably be remembered as the Second Hundred Years' War. Since August 1914 there has been a steady but shifting state of war across several continents, giving every generation a war to call its own. Never a war lover, Hemingway knew that old men start wars for their sons to fight, and he advocated executing those who started them. But if war was the milieu into which he was born, he would know it for what it was, studying its history, its tactics, and its mistakes, without ever glorifying it. Quite early he learned that neither war nor, in the long run, life itself had any winners. Countries might triumph, but one way or another, the individual was sure to lose.

Those who have not read his texts, knowing only the public icon created by the media, mistakenly believe that Hemingway wrote about winning. Nothing could be further from the truth. Early and late in his career, he wrote about men at the end of their professional lives: bullfighters, boxers, soldiers facing inevitable loss. In "Fifty Grand," boxing champion Jack Brennan, past his prime, knows that his next fight will be his last. Colonel Cantwell, the professional soldier in *Across the River and into the Trees,* maintains himself with quiet dignity, knowing that his heart is about to fail him. Manuel Garcia, who should have retired from the bullring when his reflexes slowed, goes back into the arena and is badly gored. At the end, the life is draining out of Garcia as the surgeon tries to save him. The story is called "The Undefeated." Yes, we lose, Hemingway affirms, but we can lose on our own terms. Loss is unavoidable, but we need not be defeated by it.

Just as unavoidable for Hemingway was the existential loneliness that now pervades so much of contemporary life, the loneliness that comes with the recognition of the human condition. Concomitant with that loneliness is the lack of a place called home. After leaving Oak Park, Hemingway was always on the move. Wherever he received his mail was merely a convenient base of operations. When living in Paris, he spent winters in the mountains, summers in Spain. When living in Key West, he fished out of Havana and Bimini, went west to Wyoming in the fall. When not following a migratory pattern, Hemingway was off to a war. His fiction is populated with lonely men who cannot say where home is. The most obvious place to find Nick Adams is on the road, traveling between points which may or may not be home. Thomas Hudson, sleeping on the floor of his house, his wives and children all gone or dead, has only his cats for comfort. A suicidal old man, drinking himself blind in a late-night Madrid bar, reminds the older waiter in "A Clean, Well-Lighted Place" of the "nada" that awaits him. In as early a work as *A Farewell to Arms,* when the pregnant Catherine Barkley asks Frederic Henry if he feels trapped by her condition, he replies that one always feels trapped biologically. That alienating recognition that one is trapped inside a dying animal is usually reserved for one's middle age, but Hemingway lost his sense of immortality that dark night on the Piave when the mortar shell exploded. His fiction that followed was never reassuring, never promising any transcendence. Any story followed far enough, he said, was bound to end badly.

Hemingway's fictional women fare no better than his men, a condition that has obscured the fact that they are often stronger willed than their consorts. Because Hemingway was so often married, many have assumed that he was a womanizer who had no respect for women and must have created either overly pliant or bitchy fictional women, such as Margot Macomber in "The Short Happy Life of Francis Macomber." These assumptions, like most easy generalizations, do not hold up to an examination of Hemingway's complete texts. In "The End of Something," Hemingway reverses male/female roles: Marge rows the baits out and Nick holds the fishing rod. At the end of the story, she is much the stronger character, and more honest than Nick. Brett Ashley in *The Sun Also Rises,* the epitome of the "New Woman" of the 1920s, turns men into swine, lives she as she pleases, and dominates any relationship. Catherine Barkley, who is said by some to be only an erotic male daydream, is just as war wounded as Frederic, with whom she falls desperately in love only after he reappears as wounded as her war-lost lover. If courage and grace under pressure are qualities to be admired, Catherine is far more heroic than Frederic, who does nothing courageous, makes no sacrifices for others, and is left alone at the end as the survivor. Observe the wife's behavior in "The Snows of Kilimanjaro," Pilar's dominance in *For Whom the Bell Tolls,* the quiet courage of Harry Morgan's wife, and the strength of the women in *The Garden of Eden* and *True at First Light.* These are not one-dimensional women, nor are they erotic daydreams. If their identities seem dependent upon a man, so were those of most women in the first half of the twentieth century. Hemingway never promised that he would make his readers feel better about their inheritance; he promised only to portray it honestly.

AWARDS AND RECOGNITION

1924 Editor Edward O'Brien dedicates *The Best Short Stories of 1923* to Ernest "Hemenway" (sic) and includes "My Old Man" in the anthology.

1929 *A Farewell to Arms* becomes Hemingway's first best-selling novel.

1930 Hemingway stories appear in four anthologies, and reviewers are referring to the "Hemingway school of writing." In September, the theater adaptation of *A Farewell to Arms* opens in New York.

1932 *A Farewell to Arms* is made into a movie starring Gary Cooper and Helen Hayes. *The New Yorker* publishes its first parody of Hemingway.

1937 On 8 July, Hemingway is a dinner guest at the White House for a presidential showing of *The Spanish Earth,* a documentary for which he wrote and read the narration. The 18 October issue of *Time* magazine has a Waldo Peirce painting of Hemingway on its cover.

1938 *To Have and Have Not* is banned in Detroit.

1940 *For Whom the Bell Tolls* becomes Hemingway's second best-seller and is immediately bought by Paramount Pictures for a then-record sum.

1941 Limited Editions Book Club awards Hemingway their triennial Gold Medal, presented by Sinclair Lewis. The Pulitzer Prize advisory board votes *For Whom the Bell Tolls* the best novel published in 1940, but the chairman of the board refuses to honor such a novel. No award in fiction is made this year.

1943 The movie version of *For Whom the Bell Tolls* opens, starring Gary Cooper and Ingrid Bergman.

1944 A *Saturday Review of Literature* readers' poll names Hemingway the leading American novelist. Viking Press publishes *The Portable Hemingway.*

1947 Hemingway is awarded the Bronze Star for his activities during World War II.

1952 The 1 September issue of *Life* magazine has Hemingway on the cover and prints *The Old Man and the Sea* in its entirety, selling more than five million copies. Hemingway receives the Medal of Honor from the Cuban Tourist Institute.

1953 Hemingway receives the 1952 Pulitzer Prize in fiction for *The Old Man and the Sea*.

1954 Hemingway survives two African plane crashes that make newspaper headlines worldwide. On 25 January, *Look* magazine runs its story of the safari with Ernest on the cover. In July, Cuba awards Hemingway the Order of Carlos Manuel de Cespedes. On 13 December, Hemingway is once more on the cover of *Time* magazine. Hemingway receives the Nobel Prize in literature with special reference to *The Old Man and the Sea*.

1958 The movie version of *The Old Man and the Sea* opens, starring Spencer Tracy.

1960 The 5 September issue of *Life* carries "The Dangerous Summer," Part 1, and has Hemingway once more on the cover.

1961 The story of Hemingway's suicide on 2 July is carried on the front page of newspapers worldwide. On 14 July he appears on the cover of *Life*.

After his death, Hemingway continued to be a media presence to the end of the century. A special 1990 issue of *Life* devoted to the "100 Most Important Americans of the 20th Century" had Louis Armstrong, Babe Ruth, Martha Graham, and Ernest Hemingway on the cover without identifying captions.

NOTES

1. *Oak Park Ordinances of 1916*, Oak Park Public Library.

2. Michael Reynolds, *Hemingway's Reading* (Princeton: Princeton University Press, 1981), pp. 39–43.

3. Letter from Edward Wilcox to Charles Fenton, 4 May 1952, Beinecke Library, Yale University.

4. Various high-school notebooks and papers, Hemingway Collection, John F. Kennedy Library, Boston.

HEMINGWAY AT WORK

GETTING ESTABLISHED

In January of 1919, when Ernest Hemingway returned to Oak Park, Illinois, from the Great War, he knew he was going to be a writer, but his sights were set no higher than the fiction in popular magazines such as *The Saturday Evening Post* and *Red Book*. He had not yet read Joseph Conrad, D. H. Lawrence, or Ivan Turgenev. He had not heard of James Joyce, Gertrude Stein, or Ezra Pound. He had not met Sherwood Anderson. Moving back into his old bedroom on North Kenilworth, he found copies of his high-school fiction modeled largely on Jack London stories. That spring of 1919, he wrote a story told by an experienced gambler to a much younger narrator. In the story, a card shark lures his seemingly innocent victim deeper and deeper into a high-stakes poker game. On the final call, the shark turns over four kings. The supposed victim turns over four aces. The older gambler then twists the story one more time when he tells the young narrator that when he folded his hand in the game, he held two aces of his own. The victim had outcheated the shark. Nothing in the story gave any indication of the writer Hemingway would become, but before he well understood point of view, he set up two filters between the reader and the story: the old and young narrators. He was also using an experienced tutor with a lesson to teach and a young tyro eager to learn. The narrative device would show up again when Hemingway wrote "Fifty Grand," in which Jack Brennan flagrantly fouls his opponent to make a fixed fight turn out as it should have.

Between the spring of 1919 and the fall of 1921, Hemingway continued to write clichéd stories of no particular merit about boxers, war veterans, reporters, gangsters, and card players. Nick Neroni, a promising young boxer who was a war hero, returns to Italy to join a revolutionary movement—a plot recycled eight years later in an aborted novel a character named Jimmy Breen. Punk Alford, a Kansas City newsman, carries a pistol while solving crimes that baffle the police. The dangerous killer Hands Evans is captured without a fight when he is dis-

March 1921. Hemingway sits with Hadley Richardson in the backyard of her St. Louis home. They both smoke cigarettes, very stylish for him, very liberated for her. He soon gave up tobacco. Like his nurse in Milan with whom he fell in love, Hadley was eight years older than Ernest. From a respected St. Louis family, Hadley had a small trust fund left to her by her late mother. She and Ernest married in September and honeymooned in the Hemingway cottage on Walloon Lake.

tracted by an opera record playing on the phonograph. A young war hero cannot impress his father until he goes back in the boxing ring to win the championship, or, in another story, cannot marry the young lovely until he wins the championship. The stories went out to the magazines but brought only rejection slips.

By the fall of 1920 Hemingway was living in Chicago, where he first read F. Scott Fitzgerald's *This Side of Paradise* (1920). Over the next six months, Hemingway's fiction improved slowly but met with no acceptances. While churning out copy for the *Cooperative Commonwealth* magazine to pay his bills, Hemingway began a fragmented, jerky novel that his wife-to-be, Hadley Richardson, thought sounded a bit like Fitzgerald. During that winter of 1920–1921, Hemingway met Sherwood Anderson, who loved to talk the writing game. Anderson pointed the eager-to-learn Hemingway toward the writing of Turgenev, Joyce, and Stein. In the fall of 1921, when Anderson learned that Hemingway was about to marry and leave for Italy to write, he told his young friend that Paris was the place he needed to be. In December of 1921, Ernest and Hadley Hemingway sailed for France with Anderson's letters of introduction to Sylvia Beach, Ezra Pound, and Gertrude Stein packed in their luggage.

Operating out of Paris, Hemingway wrote freelance stories for the *Toronto Star,* and when important events in postwar Europe arose, he was frequently sent on special assignments. In this capacity he covered the Genoa Economic Conference (April 1922), the Greco-Turkish War (August–September 1922), the Lausanne Peace Conference (November–December 1922), and the French occupation of the German Ruhr (April 1923). Bonding with seasoned foreign correspondents, the novice Hemingway absorbed a rich lesson in the political realities that would shape his century. At Genoa he was among the first to see and hear the newly ascended communist diplomats from post-czarist Russia. On the plains of Thrace, he witnessed a long line of refugees, carrying what belongings were portable, struggling to find safety from their invaders: an image that would become commonplace before he died. At Lausanne, Hemingway saw the old political order trying desperately to maintain itself in a world that no longer operated as it did before the Great War. In the Ruhr, he reported on the brutal French occupation of Germany's industrial heartland, one more act assuring that another war would be fought.

Working in tandem with seasoned foreign correspondents, Hemingway learned to write quickly while frequently on the run, to observe details accurately and to question surface appearances. By the end of 1922 most of his once-flowery phrasing was reduced to straightforward, declarative sentences. But his journalistic style

"On the *Star* you were forced to learn to write a simple, declarative sentence. This is useful to anyone. Newspaper work will not harm a young writer and could help him if he gets out of it in time. This is one of the dustiest cliches there is and I apologize for it. But when you ask someone old tired questions you are apt to receive old tired answers."

Ernest Hemingway

From George Plimpton, "The Art of Fiction: Ernest Hemingway," *Paris Review*, 5 (Spring 1958): 60–89.

almost always included himself in the story as the observer, the narrator connecting the reader to the event. When his fiction matured, he would use the minor-character narrator in stories such as "The Mother of a Queen," "Fifty Grand," and "God Rest You Merry, Gentlemen." Eighteen months among the journalists who belonged to the Anglo-American Press Club in Paris left Hemingway less naive and more cynical about public figures. There is little evidence that he returned from World War I disillusioned with the war or his government, but by the end of 1923, he was transformed into a charter member of the Lost Generation, those disillusioned survivors of the World War I era.

Between January 1922 and April 1923, while writing ninety-five stories for the *Star*, Hemingway also completed a short, intense education in the foundations of modernism. Pound tutored him on the principles of imagism: direct treatment of the thing itself; no superfluous words; let images convey meaning. Gertrude Stein told him to read Gertrude Stein, to discard what he had written in Chicago and start over. At Beach's bookstore, Shakespeare and Company, he read Joyce's *Dubliners* (1914), *A Portrait of the Artist as a Young Man* (1916), and, when it came out, *Ulysses* (1922). On the walls of Stein's apartment, he saw her collection of paintings by Paul Cézanne, Georges Braque, Pablo Picasso, and Juan Gris. Within two years he knew the painters Joan Miro, Fernand Leger, Andre Masson, and Picasso. All of his European experiences—political, literary, and artistic—combined as ideal training for a talented young man in search of his writing career.

In the winter of 1922 Hemingway's Chicago novel and most of his newly written Paris stories disappeared when a train thief stole Hadley's bag that carried them. Early in 1923 Hemingway started over again, trying to write single, true sentences—"true" in the imagist's sense of bearing witness, looking for the images that defined the scene. One of them caught a well-known and much-married American beauty, emblematic of rich Americans in Paris: "I have seen Peggy Joyce at 2 A.M. in a *dancing* in the Rue Caumartin quarreling with the shellacked haired young Chilean who had long pointed finger nails, danced like Rudolph Valentino and shot himself at 3:30 that same morning."[1] He called this small collection of sentences "Paris, 1922."

By the spring of 1923 Hemingway was moving on to short, "true" paragraphs that would eventually become the vignettes of *in our time* (1924). Hemingway called them "unwritten stories," in the sense that each compressed into one page the moment of recognition, the scene that tells the reader through carefully chosen detail all he needs to know. Several of these paragraphs centered on war experiences, most of them coming from secondary sources. Here, for example, a dispassionate British voice narrates one of those moments:

"What a writer must try to do is to write as truly as he can. For a writer of fiction has to invent out of what he knows in order to make something not photographic, or naturalistic, or realistic, which will be something entirely new and invented out of his own knowledge.

"What a writer should try to do is to make something which will be so written that it will become a part of the experience of those who read him."

Ernest Hemingway

From Harvey Breit, "The Sun Also Rises in Stockholm," *New York Times Book Review*, 7 November 1954, p. 1.

> We were in a garden at Mons. Young Buckley
> came in with his patrol from across the river.
> The first German I saw climbed up over the garden wall. We waited till he got
> one leg over and then potted him. He had so much equipment on and looked
> awfully surprised and fell down into the garden. Then three more came over further down the wall. We shot them. They all came just like that.[2]

These sketches are small pieces of modern times, detached voices describing concise, frequently bloody events.

As Hemingway patiently developed and sharpened the style that would make him famous, his Paris literary connections began bringing him possibilities that, for the moment, exceeded his imagination. When Jane Heap, the co-editor of the *Little Review,* asked Hemingway to contribute to an "Exiles" issue of the avant-garde periodical, Ernest sent her the six vignettes he had finished. About the same time, Pound invited Hemingway to be one of the contributors to a project he and William Bird proposed. The previous summer, Bird, a newsman by trade and a printer by avocation, bought a hand-set printing press, establishing the Three Mountains Press. In need of something to publish, Bird asked Pound to select six authors for a series that would examine the state of contemporary English prose.

Hemingway readily agreed to be part of the project but had nothing new to offer Bird, for he had recently given all of his extant writing to another Left Bank writer and publisher, Robert McAlmon. Hemingway and McAlmon met in Rapallo, Italy, in February 1923, becoming for a short while close friends. The thin chapbook McAlmon published in August of that year was Hemingway's *Three Stories & Ten Poems,* which included "Up in Michigan," a story Stein told him could never be published because of its sexuality; "My Old Man," a racetrack story done in the manner of Sherwood Anderson; and "Out of Season," a subtle story of marital conflict. To meet his commitment to Three Mountains Press, Hemingway composed twelve more of his "unwritten stories," which Bird published as *in our time* in 1924.

Hemingway later described what he was working toward during his Paris apprenticeship:

> I was trying to write then and I found the greatest difficulty, aside from knowing truly what you really felt, rather than what you were supposed to feel, and had been taught to feel, was to put down what really happened in action; what the actual things were which produced the emotion that you experienced. . . . the sequence of motion and fact which made the emotion and which would be as valid in a year or in ten years. . . .[3]

By the time he and his pregnant wife Hadley returned to Toronto in the fall of 1923, Hemingway had, with critical input from his famous friends, methodically retrained himself as a writer. With new tools and techniques at his command, he was now ready to move from vignettes to short stories, but the birth of his first son, John, and his daily duties at the *Toronto Star* made his return to Canada a frustrating experience. Stories were forming themselves in his mind, but he had no time or energy left to write them. In January of 1924, after handing in his resignation to the *Star,* Ernest, Hadley and four-month-old John boarded a ship to return to France. Before they reached Paris, Edward O'Brien dedicated *The Best Short Stories of 1923* to "Ernest Hemenway [sic]" and included "My Old Man" in the volume.

Reestablishing himself in a Left Bank cold-water flat just off Boulevard Montparnasse, Hemingway quickly began writing the stories that would remake American short fiction. In what was nothing less than a wonder year, these stories seemed to explode onto paper, many of them with the character Nick Adams as their focal point. The first story written was "Indian Camp," in which young Nick watches his father, the Doctor, perform a cesarean section on an Indian woman, using a jackknife for a scalpel and without benefit of anesthetic. Before the night visit is done, Nick sees in the upper bunk the bloody slit throat of the woman's husband who has committed suicide with a straight razor. Rowing back across the lake in the morning light, Nick queries his father about death:

"Is dying hard, Daddy?"

"No, I think it's pretty easy, Nick. It all depends."[4]

In less than five pages, Hemingway established several themes which would occupy his attention for years to come: fathers and sons; sex and death; how to face death; the wounded man; and suicide.

Under the guise of "work in progress," "Indian Camp" was published that April in the *transatlantic review*, Ford Madox Ford's literary periodical on which Hemingway assisted as an unpaid editor. The *transatlantic* lasted only one year (1924), but it exposed Hemingway to submissions from most of the young Left Bank writers of his generation. By analyzing what was right or wrong about submitted stories, he was extending his Paris education. By the fall of 1924 Hemingway had expanded two of his vignettes, made revisions to the stories from *Three Stories & Ten Poems,* and written nine new stories, six of which featured Nick Adams in a series of archetypal situations: the son disappointed by the father; the teenager breaking up with his girlfriend; male bonding; and the young father feeling trapped by his wife's pregnancy. His gossipy column appeared semiregularly in the *transatlantic,* which also published two more of his Nick Adams stories: "The Doctor and the Doctor's Wife" and "Cross Country Snow." During 1924, several of his poems appeared in *Querschnitt,* and *Little Review* published his almost unpublishable story "Mr. and Mrs. Elliot," written in the manner of Stein.

Early December 1925. Ernest, Hadley, and their two-year-old son, John, called "Bumby," are walking a mountain road near Schruns, Austria, where they have gone to ski. Within a year the first Hemingway marriage begins to come apart. John, later called Jack, grows up with Hadley, visiting his father during vacations. Ernest gives Hadley his only possession of value at the time of their breakup: the lifetime royalties from *The Sun Also Rises.*

In August of 1924 Hemingway finished the penultimate draft of "Big Two-Hearted River," the story which would anchor the collection *In Our Time* (1925). Here Hemingway solidified all that he had learned since arriving in Paris. Using a narrowly focused third-person narrator, he wrote of Nick Adams's return to the river after the war. But the narrator never mentions the war or what happened to Nick there. It is left to the reader to discover through silences, imagery, and metaphors that

Nick Adams is attempting to rehabilitate himself. Nick watches the trout holding steady in the fast-moving water, which, by implication, is how he would like to behave under pressure. The town of Seney is burned over; nothing remains the way it was the last time Nick passed through. Grasshoppers have turned black from the fires. Nick wonders how long it will take them to return to normal. By this point, the reader senses that this is not an ordinary fishing trip. Having barely turned twenty-four, Hemingway had written a story for the ages.

In October of 1924, seven months before he met Hemingway, Fitzgerald wrote Maxwell Perkins, his editor at Scribners, about this new rising talent: "This is to tell you about a young man named Ernest Hemmingway [*sic*], who lives in Paris, (an American) writes for the transatlantic Review + has a brilliant future. . . . I'd look him up right away. He's the real thing."[5] At that same moment, Hemingway was putting the final touches to the collection of his stories that he was calling *In Our Time*. Comprised of almost everything he had written since January of 1923, the manuscript used the vignettes from *in our time* as counterpoint, one positioned between each story. The volume opens with Nick and his father rowing across the lake to the Indian Camp, and closes with Nick fishing, alone, on Big Two-Hearted River after the war. Cool, ironic, and detached, the stories raised crucial questions for the generation returning from World War I. *How should a man deal with his fears? What is the proper relationship between man and woman? Where is home, and how can I live there if I find it?* That winter, while Hemingway and his family were skiing in Schruns, Austria, his literary friends Donald Ogden Stewart and Harold Loeb were pushing his manuscript with New York publishers. Unbeknownst to any of them, Perkins was writing letters to the wrong Paris address to tell Hemingway that Scribners wanted first look at his next book. By the time Perkins made contact, Hemingway had already signed a contract with the New York publisher Boni and Liveright, whose leading author was Sherwood Anderson.

Having achieved his goal of signing with a New York publisher, Hemingway seemed to have completed his apprenticeship, but he had other lessons to learn. As soon as he signed the contract, Horace Liveright asked him to replace "Up in Michigan," which describes the loveless deflowering of Liz Coates, with a new story. It would not do, Liveright said, for Hemingway's first American book to be banned from distribution by the federal government. Disgruntled, Hemingway quickly wrote an equally dark-sided story in which Nick Adams stumbles unawares into the hobo camp of a smooth-talking black man and his ward, a punch-drunk boxer whose bouts of insanity were made worse by a failed marriage to a woman many thought to be his sister. Hemingway called it "The Battler," and Boni and Liveright accepted it, publishing 1,335 copies of *In Our Time* on 5 October 1925.

When the book appeared in Shakespeare and Company's window, Hemingway was less than thrilled. The dust jacket was so crowded with the names of boosters and their blurbs that he wondered aloud if anyone would notice he had written the book. The small print run and even smaller amount of advertising also irritated him. He may have begun as a cult writer publishing in little magazines, but he fully intended to make a living from his writing. If the first printing sold out, *In Our Time* would barely pay back the $200 advance from Liveright. Moreover, his contract had bound him to his publisher for his next three books when he received a letter from Perkins literally begging him to publish with Scribners. Fitzgerald, whom Ernest met in April 1925, told him he was a fool to publish with anyone else.

Back in the Hemingway flat were his schoolboy's notebooks filled cover to cover with a novel written during the summer of 1925. After taking friends to his third feria of San Fermín in Pamplona, Hemingway spent the next six weeks writing the sad story of Jake Barnes's hopeless love for Brett Ashley and her humiliating promiscuity with his friends. Less than three weeks before *In Our Time* was published, Hemingway finished the first draft of "Fiesta, A Novel." It was revised and published in 1926 as *The Sun Also Rises*. On the last day of September, he celebrated by buying Joan Miro's large oil painting *The Farm* as a birthday present for Hadley. The price was two thousand francs, roughly $100, or the cost of two month's rent and groceries in 1925 Paris.

Ezra Pound, Paris, 1922. Literary talent scout, editor of T. S. Eliot's *The Waste Land,* promoter of James Joyce, poet, and midwife to modern literary movements, Pound was Hemingway's early Paris mentor. Hadley remembered a visit to Pound's apartment, when he was drinking endless cups of tea and talking nonstop: "Ernest listened at E P's feet, as to an oracle, and I believe some of the ideas lasted all through his life." (Michael Reynolds, *Hemingway: The Paris Years,* p. 22)

As soon as the first reviews of *In Our Time* arrived from his New York clipping service, Hemingway was pleased that most of the important reviews were positive and that *The New York Times* said

> Hemingway has a lean, pleasing, tough resilience. His language is fibrous and athletic, colloquial and fresh, hard and clean; his very prose seems to have an organic being of its own. . . . Mr. Hemingway packs a whole character into a phrase, an entire situation into a sentence or two. He makes each word count three or four ways.[6]

But it galled him that reviewers agreed that he sounded like Sherwood Anderson with touches of Gertrude Stein. Never one to undervalue his own work, Hemingway felt with some justification that his *In Our Time* stories were better than most of Anderson's fiction, and certainly better than Anderson's *Dark Laughter* (1925), which was at the moment a best-seller for Boni and Liveright. He also knew that Stein could not have written a story like "Indian Camp."

By the end of October, with the elation of publication worn thin, Hemingway was a conflicted young man. To all his friends he was complaining that Liveright was not even trying to sell *In Our Time,* that bookstores could not get copies, that no one in Chicago, his hometown, had heard of it. Maybe Liveright was waiting on Hemingway's novel, rumors of which had already reached New York. Maybe novels sold better than stories. Certainly Liveright was making Anderson a lot of money on *Dark Laughter,* but no one in Oak Park could find a copy of *In Our Time.*[7] Boni and Liveright had him bound by contract to deliver his next book, but contracts could be broken. All Hemingway had to do was write a book that Liveright would refuse to print. From Sylvia Beach's bookshop, Ernest checked out his friend Don Stewart's *Parody Outline of History* (1921) to see what a satire might look like.

On 23 November, with his family sick with winter colds and Paris grey, chilly, and rain-swept, Hemingway began pounding out on his portable typewriter the story of Scripps O'Neil, a writer with two wives, a daughter called Lousy, and an insatiable need to wander. Alternately writing in the styles of Anderson and Stein, Hemingway called the first section "Red and Black Laughter," punctuating chapter endings with an Indian war whoop. Taking a swipe at Stein's *The Making of Americans* (1925), he labeled the last section "The Passing of a Great Race and the Making and Marring of Americans." With exaggerated name-dropping and whole paragraphs of rhetorical questions, the satire of Anderson was painfully funny. Hemingway's Steinesque paragraphs with glaring grammatical errors were equally exaggerated:

Inside the beanery. They were all inside the beanery. Some do not see the others. Each are intent on themselves, Red men are intent on red men. White men are intent on white men or white women. There are no red women. Are there no squaws any more? What has become of the squaws? Have we lost our squaws in America? Silently, through the door which she had opened, a squaw came into the room. She was clad only in a pair of worn moccasins. On her back was a papoose. Beside her walked a husky dog.[8]

In chapter-ending authorial intrusions, the narrator gives more deliberately self-conscious information: "Now I am going to write the next chapter. . . . and I think I can promise you that it will be a bully chapter. At least, it will be just as good as I can write it. We both know how good that can be, if we read the blurbs, eh, reader?" (77) Filled with non sequiturs, mysterious asides, and a banquet of literary allusions, the first draft was completed in ten days and sent to the typist under the title *The Torrents of Spring,* taken from Turgenev, of whom Anderson was so fond.

The satire was Hemingway's declaration of independence from Anderson and Stein and his contract-breaker with Liveright, who could not afford to insult his best-selling author Anderson by publishing the book. On 7 December, Hemingway put *Torrents* into the mail with a cover letter asking for a $500 advance and Liveright's assurance that he would push the book. On 31 December, Liveright cabled Hemingway: "REJECTING TORRENTS OF SPRING PATIENTLY AWAITING MANUSCRIPT SUN ALSO RISES WRITING FULLY."[9]

In February of 1926 Hemingway sailed to New York, where he faced down Liveright and walked over to Perkins's office a free man, handing Perkins the typescript of *The Torrents of Spring.* Scribners immediately offered to publish *Torrents* and the as-yet-unseen *The Sun Also Rises,* giving Hemingway a 15 percent royalty rate and an advance of $1,500 against both books. He now had the major New York publisher with whom he would continue to the end of his life.

TECHNIQUES AND REVISIONS

Although Hemingway denigrated his journalism, saying it was never written to last longer than a day or two, writing to meet deadlines taught him to observe closely and to compose quickly. By the time he began writing his breakthrough short stories in 1924, he was a seasoned journalist who could write under almost any circumstances. In Paris, he began composing with pencil or pen in notebooks (*cahiers*) used by French students, but he would also use sheets of letterhead stationery from hotels. In those early years, he frequently wrote in bed or in a café, but he had trained himself to write almost anywhere. Typically, he wrote

"After I have written a book I only wish to see it published exactly as I wrote it and have as many people read it as possible. You write for yourself and for others."

Ernest Hemingway

From Harvey Breit, "Success, It's Wonderful!" *New York Times Book Review*, 3 December 1950, p. 58.

first drafts in longhand (holograph), typed revised drafts on his portable typewriter, and had final drafts typed by a professional typist.

Unlike authors who needed quiet havens in which to write, Hemingway wrote well on the road. *The Sun Also Rises* was largely drafted in Spanish hotels while Ernest and his first wife followed the summer bullfights. *For Whom the Bell Tolls,* published in 1940, was written in a Havana hotel and a lodge at Sun Valley, Idaho. His ability to create in unfamiliar and distracting places was tested during the months that he was drafting and revising *A Farewell to Arms,* published in 1929. Begun in Paris and continued on a transatlantic voyage to Key West, the novel moved with Hemingway through the summer of 1928. From Key West to Piggott, Arkansas, and on to Kansas City, he wrote steadily while Pauline, his second wife, prepared to deliver his second child. In the Kansas City hospital Ernest watched the surgeon perform the cesarean section. At the end of July he left Pauline recuperating in Piggott while he drove to Sheridan, Wyoming, where, on 22 August, he finished his first draft, 650 handwritten pages.

Hemingway seldom planned his stories or novels out on paper. As he told George Plimpton in a 1958 interview in *The Paris Review,* "Sometimes you know the story. Sometimes you make it up as you go along and have no idea how it will come out. Everything changes as it moves."[10] There is ample evidence of Hemingway's unplanned approach to his fiction among his manuscripts at the John F. Kennedy Library in Boston. There one can read fragments—a paragraph, a page, several pages—that he began, struggled with, and dropped: stories that went nowhere. Sometimes he came back to those fragments to give them another try. Several of his finished stories developed this way: "Ten Indians," "The Sea Change," and "Fathers and Sons."

Not knowing how a fresh story would end allowed for spontaneity, but it also meant that Hemingway had to revise the beginning once he had figured out the ending. Early in his career, he would start a story thinking it was about one thing only to discover, once into it, that it was about something else. One of his earliest mature stories, "Indian Camp," originally began with a fragment, published posthumously as "Three Shots," describing the night fears of a very young Nick Adams. Once the story was finished, Hemingway prepared a typescript eliminating "Three

Shots," creating the brilliant opening: "At the lake shore there was another row boat drawn up. The two Indians stood waiting." The reader does not know what lake it is, who is speaking, or what the Indians want, but the tension is real, pulling the reader into the story. This effect was created by eliminating the first several pages of the first draft, a technique Hemingway called the iceberg effect—keeping as much of the story as possible below the surface, unwritten, giving the reader sufficient clues to understand the whole without the author explaining it. The manuscripts for "Hills Like White Elephants" provide an interesting illustration. In the first draft, the setting is established, the white hills are observed by Ernest and Hadley, and they catch the train for Madrid with other travelers. Probably written in 1925, this sketch is simply a narrative with no story, an example of Hemingway writing up an incident not knowing if it would turn into anything. Returning to the fragment in 1927, he wrote a story of a young couple discussing an abortion while waiting for the train to Madrid. All that shows above the supporting surface is the crisis of the story. Left out is both the beginning and the end, which the reader must supply. How the couple arrived at this spot in this condition is left unsaid, except for the numerous hotel stickers on their luggage. What will happen to them after they board the train is left to the reader's imagination, but from the tenor of their conversation, it seems likely this relationship will turn out badly.

During his Paris years, Hemingway's revisions were focused mainly on the way stories and novels began and ended. The middle parts, particularly the dialogue, frequently went from first draft to printed page unchanged. His tendency to write unnecessary beginnings can be seen in the draft of *The Sun Also Rises,* the opening of which was cut in galley proofs at Fitzgerald's urging. As Fitzgerald told Hemingway, the tone was wrong and the reader learned nothing that he would not be told again later. With *A Farewell to Arms* Hemingway knew exactly where the story started, with troops moving down the dusty Italian road, but, trying to tie up loose ends, he wrote past the story's natural ending. Finally, he let the story end where it should, with Frederic walking back to the hotel in the rain. Later, when finishing *For Whom the Bell Tolls,* he once more tried to write past the ending, but finally asked his editor:

> What would you think of ending the book as it ends now without the epilogue?
>
> I have written it and re-written it and it is o.k. but it seems sort of like going back into the dressing room after the fight. . . .
>
> I have a strong tendency to do that always on account of wanting everything completely knit up and stowed away ship-shape.[11]

With Perkins's agreement, Hemingway scrapped the epilogue and let the story end with Jordan sighting down the machine gun barrel at his approaching enemy.

Hemingway's revisions to his early work were of three types: elimination of excesses, sometimes whole pages; additions as short as a word and as long as several pages; and painstaking reconfigurations of descriptive paragraphs. For example, here are successive drafts of the second sentence of the opening paragraph of *A Farewell to Arms:*

A. The river ran in channels in the bed of white pebbles and white boulders and there were always troops going by the house and down the road and the dust they raised powdered the leaves of the trees.

B. The water in the river ran in clear channels

C. The river bed was white pebbles and dry white boulders and the water was clear and swiftly moving and blue in the deep channels.

D. In the bed of the river there were pebbles and boulders, dry and white in the sun, and the water was clear and swiftly moving and blue in the channels.[12]

These revisions add no essential information to the first draft; they rearrange the content rather than revise it. The several revisions to the entire paragraph follow this same pattern of rearrangement, so that the reader, in fact, knows no more about the setting in the final draft than he would have learned in the first draft. It is the poetics of the phrasing, not the content, that have been altered. The rhythm of the words is as important to Hemingway as the images themselves. At his very best, Hemingway writes with poetic cadences, bass rhythms that carry the melody.

Critical response to Hemingway's work was seldom helpful to him, for his skin was quite thin when it came to constructive criticism. When Fitzgerald advised him to cut the opening of *The Sun Also Rises,* Hemingway took the advice. Three years later, when Fitzgerald offered a lengthy critique of *A Farewell to Arms* in typescript, Hemingway ignored all of his suggestions, writing on the letter's margin, "Kiss my ass." Critical response to his first two novels was so generally positive that there was little to learn from them. During the 1930s, when the New York critics seemed to gang up on Hemingway's treatise on the bullfight, *Death in the Afternoon,* Hemingway attacked them directly in *Green Hills of Africa,* saying that writers should never read their critics:

If they believe the critics when they say they are great then they must believe them when they say they are rotten and they lose confidence. At present we have two good writers who cannot write because they have lost confidence through reading critics.[13]

However, during the 1930s, proletariat criticism, whose Marxist view favored fiction depicting the struggle of the working class, was in part responsible for Hemingway's only novel published during that decade: *To Have and Have Not.*

NOTES

1. Items 647, 647a, Hemingway Collection, John F. Kennedy Library, Boston.

2. From the revised vignette in *In Our Time* (New York: Scribners, 1930), p. 29.

3. *Death in the Afternoon* (New York: Scribners, 1932), p. 2.

4. "Indian Camp," in *The Complete Short Stories of Ernest Hemingway* (New York: Scribners, 1987), p. 70.

5. *F. Scott Fitzgerald: A Life in Letters,* edited by Matthew J. Bruccoli (New York: Scribners, 1994), p. 82.

6. *New York Times Book Review,* 18 October 1925, p. 8.

7. Ernest Hemingway to Harold Loeb, ca. early November 1925, Hemingway Collection, John F. Kennedy Library, Boston.

8. *The Torrents of Spring* (New York: Scribners, 1926), p. 78.

9. Carlos Baker, *Ernest Hemingway: A Life Story* (New York: Scribners, 1969), p. 162.

10. "Ernest Hemingway," in *Writers at Work: The Paris Review Interviews, Second Series* (New York: Viking, 1963), p. 233.

11. Ernest Hemingway to Maxwell Perkins, 26 August 1940, in *The Only Thing That Counts: The Ernest Hemingway/Maxwell Perkins Correspondence,* edited by Bruccoli (New York: Scribners, 1996), p. 291.

12. Hemingway Collection, John F. Kennedy Library, Boston.

13. *Green Hills of Africa* (New York: Scribners, 1935), p. 23.

HEMINGWAY'S ERAS

After 1921 Ernest Hemingway never lived in an American urban center, never worked nine-to-five for an American employer, never, as far as is known, voted in an election. But he paid his U.S. taxes, was a loyal American in time of war, and always thought of himself as a native son. When one speaks of Hemingway's "eras," one must realize that there are no easy generalizations. Most American writers are formed during their first twenty years, spend their apprenticeship digesting their experience, and become associated with the period of their fame. For example, few of the successful 1920s novelists with whom Hemingway is associated managed to remain successful during the Great Depression of the 1930s. Sinclair Lewis, Ben Hecht, F. Scott Fitzgerald, Thornton Wilder, Willa Cather, and Ellen Glasgow—all of whom burned brightly during the 1920s—did not fare well during the 1930s. Fewer still were able to make the transition into the postwar culture of the 1940s and 1950s. Out of that generation of novelists born around the turn of the century, only Hemingway and William Faulkner managed to write well across four decades. By the mid 1950s, these two writers, both reaching the end of their lives, dominated the American literary scene. Thus, to speak of Hemingway's "era" is to trace the cultural, social, and political currents of the first half of the twentieth century, a task that would require volumes to complete. What follows is a sketch of the three eras in which Hemingway wrote.

Because Hemingway lived out of the country between 1921 and 1929 and again between 1940 and 1960, any American cultural, social, or political forces during these thirty years affected him from a distance. Yet, he was probably far better informed than most Americans, for he regularly read several newspapers and subscribed to a broad spectrum of periodicals. Moreover, his constant and varied travels, combined with his enormous correspondence and steady stream of visitors, kept him continuously in touch with the world elsewhere. While distance from an event may make it less immediate, that same distance gives a perspective

Pamplona, Spain, July 1925. The festival of San Fermín. Ernest sits at a sidewalk cafe with an unidentified man, Lady Duff Twysden, Hadley, Donald Ogden Stewart, and Pat Guthrie. Within two weeks Hemingway began writing *The Sun Also Rises,* in which Duff became Brett Ashley and Guthrie became Mike Campbell. Stewart is one of two Hemingway friends who served as a model for the character Bill Gorton.

to the event that those on the scene lack. Hemingway had it both ways. He might be living on the outskirts of the American scene, but he made frequent forays into its heartland: New York, Los Angeles, Kansas City, Chicago, and New Orleans. Even better, he regularly drove across the country, stopping in wayside diners and small-town tourist courts where he listened to the voices of common folk.

THE PARIS YEARS: 1921–1929

It was the time of the silent movies, the time when stars were born, when Henry Ford's automobiles dominated the American road. It was the time of Prohibition, speakeasies, rumrunners, bootleggers, Al Capone, and gang wars. In the clubs, black musicians were playing hot jazz, and everyone was doing the Charleston. Young women in cloche hats and short skirts were drinking gin out of silver flasks and smoking Fatima cigarettes. That was one side of the decade that roared. Meanwhile, in Washington, D.C., the U.S. Congress passed the Palmer Acts (1919) allowing the Department of Justice to deport undesirable aliens whose citizenship mattered less than their politics. It was the country's first Red Scare. Communists were coming to take away money from the rich and turn the United States into a godless nation; several thousand naturalized immigrants were deported to their points of origin. Politicians built trade barriers to protect American goods for "one hundred percent Americans." Too late to save the fifty thousand American troops who died in the last six months of the Great War "to make the world safe for Democracy," the Republican presidents of the 1920s led the country into isolationism, calling for no more foreign wars. It was the time of the Ku Klux Klan, thousands strong, marching down Pennsylvania Avenue in Washington, D.C., in full, flowing white regalia. It was the time of "America First," of fascist groups who were free to hate those foreigners who were closest to hand. The stock market went up and up. In Boston two Italian anarchists, Sacco and Vanzetti, were arrested, tried, and found guilty of murder committed during a daylight robbery in South Braintree. Appeals were made. Hearings set. New evidence reviewed. To free the two Italians became the great liberal cause of the 1920s, and, like other liberal causes of the period, it came to nothing. The two men went to the electric chair the same year, 1927, that Charles Lindbergh flew across the Atlantic and into history.

Living as an American in Paris, Hemingway caught the scent of Greenwich Village carried into the Parisian quarter of Montparnasse by the back-and-forth ambles of New York literati, and from their Ivy League imitators who flocked into Paris every summer, lingering into the early fall. The bohemian life espoused by the Village and its Left Bank counterparts was "1) a rebellion against authority: the bohemian preferred to become a literary anarchist rather than endure an authority he did not respect; 2) an attempt, however poor, to find the ideal life and the free one—this, when the attempt was genuine and not mere faking; 3) the natural result of the defeat of respect and propriety that the war had caused."[1] The American literary and would-be literary crowd that gravitated to the Left Bank of Paris became the expatriates that American periodicals loved to admire, scorn, analyze, and bemoan until the 1929 stock-market crash sent most of them home again.

Paris of the 1920s was a haven for several American live-abroad types who were roundly satirized by a 1927 *Saturday Evening Post* half-page cartoon accompanying a Gilbert Seldes essay. A European traveler boarding a transatlantic liner is being seen off by several Americans who are variously labeled: rich idler, get-rich-promoter, snob, unappreciated genius, unsuccessful artiste, and divorcer. They tell the departing European, "You'll not like America." "No gentleman can live there." "Give my regards to the land of Volstead [name of the 1919 U.S. law enforcing prohibition]!" "I'm ashamed of my country."[2] Only two of these types (failed artiste and unappreciated genius) actually lived on the Left Bank of the Seine, while the moneyed Americans remained on the more expensive Right Bank, but sometimes slummed in the Latin Quarter clubs and cafés. As more than one insider reported, there were plenty of pretend painters and phony writers who lived in the cafés without visible means of support.

Hemingway's first glimpse of Left Bank bohemians brought out all of his Oak Park values, which were not yet acclimatized:

> The scum of Greenwich Village, New York, has been skimmed off and deposited in large ladles on that section of Paris adjacent to the Café Rotonde. . . . It is a strange-acting and strange-looking breed that crowd the tables. . . . They have all striven so hard for a careless individuality of clothing that they have achieved a sort of uniformity of eccentricity. . . . You can find anything you are looking for at the Rotonde—except serious artists . . . the artists of Paris who are turning out creditable work resent and loathe the Rotonde crowd. . . . They are nearly all loafers. . . . By talking about art they obtain the same satisfaction that the real artist does in his work.[3]

Two years later, Hemingway would be dressed just as eccentrically as any of the Rotonde crowd, talking seriously with recent arrivals from Greenwich Village.

As Hemingway was acutely aware, hardworking writers and painters lived on the Left Bank because it afforded better lodging

and food for their money than New York or Chicago. The editorialist for *The Literary Digest* rhetorically asked, "Where in America can you find a suit of clothes, which even a Greenwich Village poet would wear, for $13.60?"[4] One of Hemingway's earliest feature stories sent back to Toronto was headlined "Living on $1,000 a Year in Paris," and his first apartment, a second-floor walk-up in a working-class neighborhood, cost Fr250 a month, or less than twenty American dollars. By the time he left Paris, seven years later, the dollar in francs was worth twice as much as it had been in 1922. By 1928, one did not need to speak French to live comfortably on the Left or Right Banks of the river, for there were fifty thousand Americans registered as Parisian residents, and several thousands of tourists arriving each summer. There was an American Hospital as well as American churches of most denominations. One could eat American food in the cafés, read American periodicals, and bank at American banks.

No matter how many American churches appeared in Paris, they could not diminish the rich sexual ambiance of the City of Lights. As Hemingway learned early in the city, relationships were seldom simple, and the possibilities for coupling began to fascinate him. Wherever he looked, men and women were operating beyond the paling of Oak Park barricades. The longer he looked the more interested he became, until his Oak Park mores became less inhibiting. Lesbian couples, for example, were an important part of Left Bank literary life. Gertrude Stein and her companion, Alice B. Toklas, were the most prominent, but there were also Margaret Anderson and Jane Heap, editors of *Little Magazine* and frequent visitors to Paris; Sylvia Beach and Adrienne Monier; Janet Flanner and her friend Solita Solano; Natalie Barney and Romaine Brooks—to name a few who were reasonably well known to Hemingway. More complicated were relationships such as that of the bisexual Robert McAlmon, who was married to "a lesbian named Winifred who called herself Bryher. As long as they remained married, McAlmon received a handsome allowance from Bryher's father. All the while, Bryher lived very quietly at Territet, Switzerland with Ezra [Pound]'s old girl friend Hilda Doolittle, who had a child fathered perhaps by D. H. Lawrence."[5]

At the Jeu de Palm and the Orangerie, Hemingway studied the Cézanne paintings; at Sylvia Beach's bookstore he read the latest copies of *Dial* magazine from New York and checked out more translations of the Russian writers suddenly in vogue. With equal intensity, he studied the racing forms and the performances of the horses at the Auteuil and Enghien courses. Later he wrote:

> You had to watch a jumping race from the top of the stands at Auteuil and it was a fast climb up to see what each horse did and see the horse that might have won and did not, and see why or maybe how he did not do what he could have done. You watched the prices and all the shifts of odds each time a horse you were following would start, and you had to know how he was working and finally get to know when the stable would try with him.[6]

There were always two sides to Hemingway's interests: contemplative and active. He was an avid reader and an avid fisherman. He was equally at home with James Joyce and Ezra Pound as he was with the jockeys at Auteuil. In Paris he regularly attended the six-day bike races and the boxing matches at Salle Wagram. He was also a regular in Gertrude Stein's salon and at Ford Madox Ford's parties.

To speak of Hemingway's Paris years is somewhat misleading, for he was constantly on the move, traveling, fishing, hiking, reporting, skiing, visiting in other countries. During his first four years in Paris, he was only in residence half the time. Every July, he and Hadley went to Spain for the feria of San Fermín at Pamplona and then on to Valencia for more corridas. Every winter they returned to the ski slopes of Austria. Wherever he traveled, his quick ear picked up language with some dexterity. Before he returned to America at the end of the 1920s, he could carry on conversations in French, Spanish, and Italian. He spoke a smattering of German and could read French and Spanish newspapers. He knew the customs of the countries in which he traveled, knew their wines and their foods, their railroads and their hotels. He prided himself on getting good value for his money wherever he went. Local interests inevitably interested him. The placidity of the Swiss, the arrogance of the Italian fascists, the intensity of Spanish politics were grist for his mill and food for his mind.

In Spain, Hemingway studied the bullfights the way some men back home were studying the stock market. He quickly absorbed the ritual three-act drama and its attendant revelry. The raw, primitive power of the fighting bull, the grace and courage of a great torero (bullfighter), the beauty and flow of the cape as the classic passes were made, and always the possibility of physical damage or death passing beneath the outstretched arm—all of these elements made other spectator events pale by

"He was unquestionably a genius, but of the kind that advertises its limits. Critics were on to these from the very beginning, but in the forward-looking 1920s, they joined his readers to make him the writer for their time. His stuff was new. It moved. There was on every page of clear prose an implicit judgment of all other writing. The Hemingway voice hated pretense and cant and the rhetoric they rode in on."

E. L. Doctorow

From "Braver Than We Thought," *The New York Times Book Review*, 18 May 1986, pp. 1, 44-45.

comparison. As soon as he returned from his first Pamplona feria, he wrote an old friend:

> 5 days of bull fighting dancing all day and all night . . . drums, reed pipes, fifes—faces of Velasquez's drinkers (?), Goya and Greco faces, all in the men in blue shirts and red handkerchiefs. . . . There were 8 of the best toreros in Spain and 5 of them got gored! . . . It isn't just brutal like they always told us. It's a great tragedy—and the most beautiful thing I've ever seen and takes more guts and skill and guts again than anything possibly could. It's just like having a ringside seat at the war with nothing going to happen to you.[7]

Two years later, in his first letter to Maxwell Perkins at Scribners, and before he had written anything longer than a short story, Hemingway hoped that he would one day be able to write a huge history of the bullfight illustrated with wonderful photographs. By the time he did (*Death in the Afternoon,* published in 1932), he saw clearly how the matador's performance in the ring brought the active life and artistic life into a single moment. "Bullfighting," he wrote, "is the only art in which the artist is in danger of death and in which the degree of brilliance in the performance is left to the fighter's honor."[8]

In December 1921 Hemingway, newly married, arrived in Paris as green as the greenest American tourist. Twenty-one years old, a wounded veteran out of the Great War, he had not yet written a single story that a magazine would buy. He knew no one in Paris, had not heard about Pamplona, and his only second language was a smattering of Italian. On 10 January 1930, when Hemingway left Paris as his principal residence to return to America, the stock market was dropping like a stone, paper profits evaporating. The young author was returning as an astute observer of European politics, including the devastated German economy, the rise of fascism, and various Spanish revolutionary factions. In the space of eight years, he had taught himself how to write, learned new languages, met the important writers of his generation, and was well on his way to becoming the legendary Hemingway. Two years married to his second wife, Hemingway returned to America with two sons, one by each wife, a newly professed Catholic religion, and two volumes of short stories, one satire, and two novels to his name. His story "The Killers" was being anthologized for college students to study. *The Sun Also Rises* and *A Farewell to Arms* were destined to become classic American novels. He was not yet thirty years old.

THE KEY WEST YEARS: 1930–1939

By 1930 American movies had learned to talk, and the American economy was spiraling downward into the worst depression the country had ever endured. Herbert Hoover, the last Republican president for twenty-two years, was trying to assure the country that the downturn was temporary as factories began to close and jobs disappeared. To worsen the situation, a crippling drought began to spread across the plains states, with dust clouds sometimes blotting out the sun. Rural banks across the country began closing their doors, unable to refund deposits to bewildered citizens. Good times and bad always cycle, the politicians said. Four million people may be out of work, but work will return. It always returns, Republicans promised. Any public relief program, according to President Hoover, was indefensible, for "federal aid for the distressed would strike at the root of government." He was certain that the Red Cross could "take care of the drought and the unemployment situation." And to prove it he gave $7,500 to the Red Cross relief fund.[9]

Inadvertently, by taking up residence on the remote, southernmost point of the United States, Key West, Florida, Hemingway positioned himself at ringside to study the effects of the Great Depression on small-town America. By February 1931 the town was on the verge of bankruptcy, unable to collect enough taxes to pay the firefighters, whose intent to walk out was a serious threat to a wooden, windswept town. The firemen compromised, taking $25 and a promise of more when tax collection improved, which it never did. With a delinquent tax sale hanging over several Key West homes, fear of displacement was real.[10] What once was a thriving fishing port with an active sponge trade and several prosperous cigar factories had fared poorly during the 1920s. The sponge beds disappeared, the factories closed down, and half the population had left the island. The depression of the 1930s was the death knell for the Key West of old.

Across America the Depression took its toll. Suicides rose dramatically. Ramshackle cardboard and rusty tin villages called Hoovervilles sprang up on the outskirts of industrial centers. Hoover wagons were broken-down cars pulled by horses or mules. Hoover blankets were newspapers spread on park benches. In newspapers, magazines, and newsreels, the black-and-white images of unemployment lines, soup kitchens, and disheartened Americans proliferated. Towering clouds of dust storms loomed over small, bleak towns on the Great Plains. Soon the roads west were littered with abandoned detritus, lonely graves, and last week's campfires left behind by "Okies" traveling to California in search of work. Their rattletrap automobiles broke down to be fixed with bailing wire and native ingenuity. At the end of the 1930s, John Steinbeck captured the times in his heartbreaking novel, *The Grapes of Wrath* (1939). In 1933, Hemingway described Nick Adams's drive cross-country, passing through a small rural community "along the empty brick-paved street, stopped by traffic lights that flashed on and off on this traffic-less Sunday, and would be gone next year when the payments on the system were not met."[11]

On the Fourth of July 1934 the citizens of Key West celebrated with a parade, footraces, a bathing beauty contest, fish fries, and fireworks, trying to ignore the fact that they could not pay their property taxes and could not afford new license plates, and that their city was in default on its municipal bonds. The next morning the headlines of the *Key West Citizen* read:

KEY WEST NOW UNDER STATE CONTROL

PASSES INTO HANDS OF FERA

IN REHABILITATION PROGRAM

STATE ADMINISTRATOR JULIUS F. STONE ACCEPTS

GOVERNOR SHOLTZ'S INVITATION TO TAKE

CHARGE OF AFFAIRS IN EMERGENCY OPERATIONS

With no means to restore Key West's original industries, the Federal Emergency Relief Administration (FERA) decided to turn the island into a tourist resort. Connected to the mainland by the Overseas Railroad and a series of ferries that tied the keys together, the island had the right climate, good beaches, and magnificent sunsets.

While Key West embraced the federal aid, renaming a principal street Roosevelt Boulevard, Hemingway was appalled by the government intrusion. When the narrator of *Green Hills of Africa* is asked by the white hunter, "What's going on in America?" he replies, "Damned if I know! Some sort of Y.M.C.A. show. Starry eyed bastards spending money that somebody will have to pay. Everybody in our town quit work to go on relief. Fishermen all turned carpenters. Reverse of the Bible."[12] Raised among the Progressive Republicans of Oak Park, Hemingway was sympathetic to the destitute of Key West, but he put his faith in the ability of local institutions to care for their own. He also had a healthy distrust of government agencies ever acting in his best interests. In 1935, when the FERA published a tourist guide-map to Key West, Hemingway, with justification, felt his privacy was being sacrificed to bolster the recovery plan for the city. His *Esquire* essay was a satirical response to the map:

> The house at present occupied by your correspondent is listed as number eighteen in a compilation of the forty-eight things for a tourist to see in Key West. So there will be no difficulty in a tourist finding it . . . a map has been prepared by the local FERA authorities to be presented to each arriving visitor.

He had no desire, he wrote, to compete with the Sponge Loft, the Turtle Crawl, the Ice Factory, or even the abandoned Cigar Factory. "Yet there your correspondent is at number 18 between Johnson's Tropical Grove (number 17) and Lighthouse and Aviaries (number 19). This is all very flattering to the easily bloated ego . . . but very hard on production."[13]

Of Hemingway's contemporaries in the 1920s, few continued writing well in the 1930s. F. Scott Fitzgerald's long-anticipated *Tender Is the Night* (1934) came too late for an audience no longer interested in the problems of rich Americans on the Riviera. John Dos Passos finished his *U.S.A.* trilogy of novels in 1936, but moved further to the political right as his readers moved to the left. William Faulkner, who was never a best-seller in the 1920s, continued to write brilliant novels, climaxing with a masterpiece, *Absalom, Absalom!* (1936); yet, he would not find his audience until the next decade. The detective fictions of Dashiell Hammett (*The Maltese Falcon,* 1930, and *The Thin Man,* 1932); the tough, sensual novels of James M. Cain (*The Postman Always Rings Twice,* 1934); and Erskine Caldwell's steamy novels about Southern sharecroppers (*Tobacco Road,* 1932) were more in tune with the 1930s.

Pamplona, Spain. Encierro, the running of the bulls. "Then they came in sight. Eight bulls galloping along, full tilt, heavyset, black, glistening, sinister, their horns bare, tossing their heads. . . . They ran in a solid mass, and ahead of them sprinted, tore, ran and bolted the rear guard of the men and boys of Pamplona who had allowed themselves to be chased through the streets for a morning's pleasure." (Hemingway, *Dateline: Toronto,* p. 349)

The proletariat writers of the Great Depression who focused on the plight of downtrodden urban industrial workers, textile mill strikes, and the urban poor had plenty to write about, but their names and the novels did not last out the decade. Their Marxist agenda, which for a while dominated the New York critical scene, was never embraced by the American working class. In *To Have and Have Not,* published in 1937,

"Everyone has his own conscience and there should be no rules about how a conscience should function. All you can be sure about in a political-minded writer is that if his work should last you will have to skip the politics when you read it. Many of the so-called politically enlisted writers change their politics frequently."

Ernest Hemingway

From George Plimpton, "The Art of Fiction: Ernest Heming-way," *Paris Review,* 5 (Spring 1958): 60–89.

Hemingway satirized such novelists with the character Richard Gordon, who was going to write a novel about a textile strike while being completely out of touch with the working class. But, for the first time, working-class characters played a major role in his fiction. With fierce self-reliance, Harry Morgan, who refuses to go on the government dole, struggles to keep his family in food. The drunken vets in the Saturday night barroom, the out-of-work fishermen, and the communist agitator who refuses to talk to Gordon are all potential mouthpieces for proletarian ideas, but truer, perhaps, to reality, they are more interested in survival than in politics. In one of his *Esquire* "letters," Hemingway spelled out his feelings about politically driven novelists:

> Now a writer can make himself a nice career while he is alive by espousing a political cause, working for it, making a profession of believing in it. . . . [But] anybody is cheating who takes politics as a way out. It is too easy. . . . don't let them suck you in to start writing about the proletariat, if you don't come from the proletariat, just to please the recently politically enlightened critics. In a little while these critics will be something else.[14]

When it seemed as if capitalism was self-destructing as Marxists had predicted, political theorists and leftist agitators were certain the revolution had come to America. But when the Stalinist purges of the mid 1930s in Russia disillusioned the would-be revolutionists, they had to admit that out-of-work Americans were not going to be swayed by dialectics alone. Food first, then ideas. Conservative politicians continued to raise the specter of communism as an internal threat to the nation, pointing to the labor unions as examples of bolshevism at work. Meanwhile, fascism here and abroad became more and more attractive to those right of center.

World War II was ready to start, but the West tried to ignore it. Americans as prominent as Joseph Kennedy, then ambassador to the Court of St. James's in England, counseled President Roosevelt to support Hitler's demands in Europe, for he was the future. In Germany the economy was healthy, and the populace was united. After close-up inspections of Germany's new air force, Charles Lindbergh gave Roosevelt much the same advice: if war broke out in Europe, Germany would be the victor. "America First" became the watchword of those who wanted no more foreign entanglements. Hemingway, who understood what was happening in Europe, told his readers: "We were fools to be sucked in once on a European war and we should never be sucked in again."[15]

In 1936 Roosevelt was reelected president of the United States. That same year, General Francisco Franco led the Spanish fascists into a civil war to overthrow the elected socialist government of the country, and Nazi troops marched unimpeded into the Rhineland, reoccupying traditionally German territory that was given to France at the end of the last war. With both Germany and Italy assisting Franco's forces, the United States stood firm on its Neutrality acts of 1935 and 1936, refusing to become involved. While American volunteers manned the Abraham Lincoln Brigade, fighting in support of the socialist government, Hemingway reported on the war as a prelude of things to come: atrocities, betrayals, and air raids on the civilian population. With an eye trained to capture the telling detail, he told American readers what it was like for civilians to live under enemy fire: "A motor car coming along the street stopped suddenly and swerved after the bright flash and roar and the driver lurched out, his scalp hanging down over his eyes, to sit down on the sidewalk with his hand against his face, the blood making a smooth sheen down over his chin."[16] In Spain, Hemingway worked closely with director Joris Ivens in the making of his documentary *The Spanish Earth,* released in 1937. When the movie was edited, Hemingway wrote the narration, which he himself read in the final cut of the picture. *The New York Times* of 21 August 1937 found Hemingway's voice-over "terse, powerful, it is vengeful, bitter and unreasoning . . . . a definitely [*sic*] propaganda effort." In a rare public appeal, Hemingway accompanied the documentary to Hollywood, where it was used to raise money for Spanish ambulances. The following year, Hemingway wrote *The Fifth Column,* a play about an undercover counterintelligence agent posing as an American journalist in Madrid during the shelling of that capital city. Foreseeing the Spanish conflict as the harbinger of wars to come, journalist Philip Rawlings prophesizes with uncanny accuracy: "We're in for fifty years of undeclared wars and I've signed up for the duration."[17]

In 1937–1938, while Hemingway was in Spain covering the civil war, the Japanese army invaded China, beginning the war on the Pacific rim. The following year, Hitler demanded Austria and the German-speaking parts of Czechoslovakia, which neither England nor France had the fortitude to deny him. Each of his demands was acceded to in the hope that he would be satisfied. On 1 September 1939 the Nazi blitzkrieg of Poland put all such hopes asunder. By the fall of 1940, the superior German army had rolled across most of western Europe, and the Luftwaffe was systematically bombing the heartland of England. President

Roosevelt, campaigning for an unprecedented third term in office, promised American mothers that not one of their sons would die on foreign soil. While western Europe and southern China reverberated with the sounds of war, Hemingway holed up in Cuba to write *For Whom the Bell Tolls*, which reminded readers that the death bell and the bells of war were tolling for all of them.

WORLD WAR II: 1940–1945

At the end of January 1941 Ernest Hemingway and his new wife, Martha Gellhorn, departed from San Francisco bound for Asia to report on the Japan-China war, she for *Collier's* magazine and he for the North American News Alliance. Before they left, they were briefed by the U.S. State Department and officers from navy intelligence, who instructed them on the kinds of helpful information they should try to bring back. At Hong Kong, Chungking, the front lines deep in south China, and along the Burma Road, the two Americans wrote their news stories and kept their eyes open for useful political intelligence. When they returned in June, they were debriefed by navy intelligence, and Hemingway later wrote Roosevelt cabinet member Henry Morgenthau a long analysis of the internal Chinese conflict between Chiang Kai-shek's nationalists and the communist rebels, temporarily united in their fight with Japan but certain to be at each other's throats when Japan was driven out of China.

By the time the Hemingways returned from Asia, America was rearming itself for a war that was not yet popular but seemed more and more inevitable. President Roosevelt reversed himself on the Neutrality acts in order to send war materials to Russia and England. The FBI turned its attention from gangsters and communists to Nazi spies and fascist organizations. On 7 December 1941 the Japanese carrier-based attack on Pearl Harbor sank the heart of the United States Pacific fleet. The U.S.S. *Arizona* along with seven other battleships and ten other naval vessels were sunk or badly damaged. Hickam Field and its aircraft were bombed out, and Schofield Barracks was filled with wounded soldiers. When the smoke cleared, two hundred American planes were smoldering, and three thousand men were dead or wounded.

Quite suddenly "America First" no longer had much meaning. On 8 December the U.S. Congress declared war on Japan. Three days later, Germany and Italy joined their axis partner Japan by declaring war on the United States. Young men, whose president once promised they would never die on foreign soil, were about to leave home, many for the first and last time. The generation who came of age with the

Austria, March 1926. Left to right: an Austrian ski instructor, Hemingway, John Dos Passos, and Gerald Murphy high above Schruns on the Silveratta. Ernest had recently returned from New York, where he signed a contract with Scribners to publish *The Torrents of Spring* and *The Sun Also Rises.*

Great European War (1914–1918) was leading its children into another one, a war that would once more change the surface of American society. Before the war ended, sixteen million Americans had been in uniform, and half a million were buried beneath white stone crosses.

In the spring of 1942 German submarines began a concentrated attack on American shipping lanes vital to the supply of oil and aluminum. With the nation unprepared to counter undersea warfare, the U-boats had easy pickings that first year of the war, sinking 243 oil tankers and freighters in the Caribbean and another hundred in the Gulf of Mexico. More ships went down off Cape Hatteras, which was a virtual shooting gallery for the U-boats. Operating far from any supply base, the German submarines enjoyed incredible success, raising suspicions that they were being aided in the waters surrounding Cuba by Spanish Falangists. In late spring of 1942, at the request of the American ambassador to Cuba, Hemingway employed bartenders, jai alai players, and others to collect intelligence on the Falangists, which he funneled back to Ambassador Braden, who in turn conveyed the information to the State Department in Washington, D.C.

Meanwhile, American and America-bound tankers and freighters continued to be sunk faster than they could be replaced. Taking emergency stopgap measures, the U.S. Navy commissioned more than a thousand private yachts and powerboats to patrol along the east coast. In Havana, Hemingway volunteered his fishing boat, *Pilar,* for such sea duty, principally along the northeast coast of Cuba. In 1943–1944, when the U.S. Navy's antisubmarine warfare caught up with the U-boats, Germany turned its raiders into wolf packs hunting in the North Atlantic shipping lanes, and Hemingway gave up his patrols to become a frontline correspondent for *Collier's* magazine.

He arrived in London in mid May 1944, barely in time to take part in the 6 June D-day invasion on the beaches of Normandy. From a landing craft taking soldiers into the Fox Green sector of Omaha Beach, Hemingway observed the landing at close quarters and reported it with his customary detail, showing his reader the confusion and pain of the invasion. Approaching another landing craft,

> I saw a ragged shellhole through the steel plates forward of her pilothouse where an 88-mm. German shell had punched through. Blood was dripping from the shiny edges of the hole into the sea with each roll of the LCI [Landing Craft Infantry]. Her rails and hull had been befouled by seasick men, and her dead were laid forward of her pilothouse.[18]

By March 1945, when Hemingway returned to Cuba, he had survived several near-death experiences, briefly commanded French Resistance fighters, been present at the liberation of Paris, and lived through three weeks of battle at Hürtgenwald where the 22nd Infantry regiment had 85 percent of its original company killed, wounded, or missing in action. At the end of April 1945 Hitler committed suicide in his Berlin bunker, and on 7 May Germany surrendered unconditionally. On 6 August the first atomic bomb was detonated over the Japanese city of Hiroshima; three days later a second atom bomb destroyed Nagasaki. Japan quickly agreed to an unconditional surrender.

THE CUBAN YEARS: 1945–1962

Although he would publish two novels after 1945 and be awarded the Pulitzer and Nobel prizes in literature, Hemingway's eras were essentially complete with the end of World War II. At age forty-five, he had absorbed the various cultural forces from the first half of the century, and now he was more interested in the past than the future. The complex and frequently corrupt Cuban politics continued to interest him, as did the continuous climate of revolution in the Caribbean. In 1947 Hemingway left Cuba just ahead of police investigators who wanted to question him about his alleged participation in an attempt to overthrow Rafael Trujillo, the dictator of the Dominican Republic. Other than infrequent visits to New York en route to Europe and cross-country drives to Idaho, Hemingway was seldom in the United States during the postwar period. When not in Cuba, he traveled extensively in Europe, principally in Italy, France, and Spain. In 1953–1954 he was on safari in Africa. It was not until the Castro revolution succeeded that Hemingway took up what he thought would be temporary residence in Ketchum, Idaho, in 1960. By that time his failing health and his terrible depressions made cultural currents largely irrelevant. He did, however, remain current in postwar fiction, without much caring for what he read. Irwin Shaw's *The Young Lions* (1948), Norman Mailer's *The Naked and the Dead* (1948), and James Jones's *From Here to Eternity* (1951) were all read with a hostile eye toward young writers encroaching on his territory.

NOTES

1. Frederick J. Hoffman, *The Twenties: American Writing in the Postwar Decade,* revised edition (New York: Free Press, 1965), pp. 39–40.

2. Gilbert Seldes, "Uneasy Chameleons," *Saturday Evening Post* (1 January 1927): 21.

3. "American Bohemians in Paris," *Toronto Star Weekly* (25 March 1922); reprinted in *Dateline: Toronto,* by Hemingway, edited by William White (New York: Scribners, 1985), pp. 114–115.

4. "Whom Has America Failed," *Literary Digest* (26 May 1928): 24.

5. Michael Reynolds, *Hemingway: The Paris Years* (Oxford & New York: Blackwell, 1989), p. 33.

6. *A Moveable Feast* (New York: Scribners, 1964), p. 62.

7. Ernest Hemingway to William D. Horne, 17–18 July 1923, in *Ernest Hemingway: Selected Letters 1917–1961,* edited by Carlos Baker (New York: Scribners, 1981), p. 88.

8. *Death in the Afternoon* (New York: Scribners, 1932), p. 91.

9. *Key West Citizen,* 3 & 10 February 1931.

10. *Key West Citizen,* January–February 1931.

11. "Fathers and Sons," in *The Complete Short Stories of Ernest Hemingway* (New York: Scribners, 1987), p. 369.

12. *Green Hills of Africa* (New York: Scribners, 1935), p. 191.

13. "The Sights of Whitehead Street: A Key West Letter," *Esquire* (April 1935); reprinted in *By-Line: Ernest Hemingway,* edited by White (New York: Scribners, 1967), p. 192.

14. "Old Newsman Writes: A Letter from Cuba," *Esquire* (December 1934); reprinted in *By-Line,* pp. 183–184.

15. "Notes on the Next War: A Serious Topical Letter," *Esquire* (September 1935); reprinted in *By-Line,* p. 212.

16. North American News Alliance dispatch (11 April 1937); reprinted in *By-Line,* p. 259.

17. *The Fifth Column and Four Stories of the Spanish Civil War* (New York: Scribners, 1969), p. 80.

18. "Voyage to Victory," *Collier's* (22 July 1944); reprinted in *By-Line,* p. 351.

Three Stories & Ten Poems. Paris: Contact Publishing Company, 1923. Robert McAlmon was the owner and editor of Contact. The stories are "Up in Michigan," "Out of Season," and "My Old Man." The last two reappeared in the 1925 story collection *In Our Time*. "Up in Michigan" was not reprinted until 1938 in a revised form.

in our time. Paris: Three Mountains Press, 1924. William Bird was the owner and editor of Three Mountains Press. This edition includes eighteen vignettes, most of which were reprinted as divisions between stories in the 1925 story collection *In Our Time*.

In Our Time. New York: Boni & Liveright, 1925. This collection includes fourteen of Hemingway's breakthrough short stories, including "Indian Camp," "The Doctor and the Doctor's Wife," "The Battler," "The End of Something," and "Big Two-Hearted River." This book was reissued by Charles Scribner's Sons in 1930 with minor revisions and one new story, "On the Quai at Smyrna," which Hemingway wrote in lieu of an author's introduction.

The Torrents of Spring. New York: Charles Scribner's Sons, 1926. A satire on the state of contemporary fiction, Sherwood Anderson, and Gertrude Stein, among other targets. This book is the contract breaker that Charles Scribner's Sons published in order to get *The Sun Also Rises*.

The Sun Also Rises. New York: Charles Scribner's Sons, 1926. Narrated by Jake Barnes, a sexually maimed World War I veteran, the story follows a group of British and American expatriates from the Left Bank of Paris to the festival of San Fermín in Pamplona, Spain. The conflict is provided by Brett Ashley, in pursuit of whom the men frequently behave badly. The local color in Paris and Spain is authentic; the characters represent the generation physically and emotionally wounded by the Great War.

Hemingway and his second wife, Pauline Pfeiffer. Four years older than he and with a substantial income, Pauline married Ernest on 10 May 1927 in Paris. She was working for *Vogue* magazine when they met. For the next ten years of their marriage, she was his best critic, his social secretary, and his manager. She and Hemingway were the parents of two sons: Patrick, born in 1928; and Gregory, born in 1931.

Men Without Women. New York: Charles Scribner's Sons, 1927. The second major collection of Hemingway's short stories, including "Hills Like White Elephants," "The Killers," "In Another Country," and "Now I Lay Me."

A Farewell to Arms. New York: Charles Scribner's Sons, 1929. Hemingway's first best-selling novel; narrated by Lieutenant Frederic Henry, an American volunteer driving ambulances for the Italian army during World War I. Frederic explains how he was wounded, fell in love with his hospital nurse (Catherine Barkley), deserted the army during the infamous retreat from Caporetto, and fled to Switzerland with the pregnant Catherine. In a difficult childbirth necessitating a cesarean delivery, the baby is born dead and Catherine hemorrhages to death. Frederic is left alone, in a neutral country, walking back to the hotel in the rain.

Death in the Afternoon. New York: Charles Scribner's Sons, 1932. Hemingway's natural history of the bullfight, its elements, participants, and evolution. Interlarded with his analysis of the corrida are numerous comments and sidelights on the profession of writing, many of them humorous. Included in the text is "A Natural History of the Dead," which reappeared in his next volume of stories.

Winner Take Nothing. New York: Charles Scribner's Sons, 1933. Hemingway's last major collection of short stories, including "A Clean, Well-Lighted Place," "A Way You'll Never Be," and "Fathers and Sons."

FROM A REVIEW OF *MEN WITHOUT WOMEN*

"I think it is impossible for him to write of any event at which he has not been present; his is, then, a reportorial talent, just as Sinclair Lewis's is. But, or so I think, Lewis remains a reporter and Hemingway stands a genius because Hemingway has an unerring sense of selection. He discards details with a magnificent lavishness; he keeps his words to their short path. His is, as any reader knows, a dangerous influence. The simple thing he does looks so easy to do. But look at the boys who try to do it."

Dorothy Parker

From *The New Yorker* (29 October 1927): 92–94.

Green Hills of Africa. New York: Charles Scribner's Sons, 1935. Hemingway's mostly nonfiction account of his African safari with a character like himself narrating a highly structured account of a competitive kudu hunt in which he is bested by another hunter. In the text are running commentaries on the art of fiction, great writers of the past, the problems of being a contemporary writer, and the impact of the Great Depression on America. As much about aesthetics as about hunting, *Green Hills of Africa* affirms Hemingway's belief that pursuit is happiness.

To Have and Have Not. New York: Charles Scribner's Sons, 1937. An experimental novel, told in several different voices and set in Key West during the Great Depression. The major characters include fishing guide and sometime rumrunner Harry Morgan and the proletarian novelist Richard Gordon. Supporting characters include the have-not fishermen of Key West, the displaced and drunken army veterans working on the overseas highway, and the rich yacht owners who anchor in the harbor. In the course of the novel, Gordon loses his wife through his liaison with the rich Helene Bradley, and Harry Morgan loses his life but not before killing the Cuban revolutionists who robbed the Key West bank.

FROM A REVIEW OF *TO HAVE AND HAVE NOT*

"So far none of Ernest Hemingway's characters has had any more consciousness than a jaguar. They are physiological systems organized around abdomens, suprarenal glands, and genitals. They are sacs of basic instinct. Their cerebrums have highly developed motor areas but are elsewhere atrophied or vestigial. Their speech is rudimentary, they have no capacity for analytical or reflective thought, they have no beliefs, no moral concepts, no ideas. Living on an instinctual level, they have no complexities of personality, emotion, or experience."

Bernard DeVoto

From "Tiger, Tiger!" *Saturday Review of Literature,* 16 (16 October 1937): 8.

The Fifth Column and the First Forty-Nine Stories. New York: Charles Scribner's Sons, 1938. The final collection of Hemingway short stories published during his lifetime. The opening play, *The Fifth Column,* is the dramatic Spanish Civil War story of Philip Rawlings, a war correspondent by day and a Loyalist counterspy by night. With him in besieged Madrid is Dorothy Bridges, a correspondent who is less committed to the Spanish cause. The play is followed by forty-nine short stories, all but five of which appeared in earlier collections. The additional stories include "Up in Michigan," "The Short Happy Life of Francis Macomber," and "The Snows of Kilimanjaro."

For Whom the Bell Tolls. New York: Charles Scribner's Sons, 1940. Hemingway's enormous best-selling novel set in the Spanish Civil War. Robert Jordan, an American saboteur, is sent behind enemy lines to destroy a crucial bridge at the beginning of a Loyalist offensive in the Guadarrama Mountains of Spain. During the three days that the novel encompasses, Jordan enlists the aid of a band of partisans led by Pablo and his dominant consort, Pilar. Jordan falls in love with a young Spanish girl, Maria, engineers the destruction of the bridge, and is badly wounded in the aftermath. Choosing to be left behind as a rear guard, he sends Maria to safety while he steels himself to delay the approaching enemy with his machine gun. Embedded in the novel are several tangential stories, narratives told by the different characters.

Across the River and into the Trees. New York: Charles Scribner's Sons, 1950. Set in Venice, Italy, the novel covers the last three days of Colonel Richard Cantwell's life, which are spent in the company of a young Venetian beauty, Renata, to whom he tells his fragmented story of what happened to him during World War II. Politically embittered by the politics of war, Cantwell lives his brief time with Renata as existentially as possible.

The Old Man and the Sea. New York: Charles Scribner's Sons, 1952. Hemingway's all-time best-selling story of Santiago, the Cuban fisherman whose epic three-day battle with a gigantic marlin can be read both as tragedy and allegory. Told from the old fisherman's point of view, the long struggle provides time for flashbacks to earlier events, sustaining memories, and dreams. Like many of Hemingway's characters, Santiago is doomed to lose, but he loses on his own terms.

POSTHUMOUS PUBLICATIONS

At his death on 2 July 1961, Hemingway left several manuscripts in various stages of completion. With the publication of *True at First Light* (1999), his literary estate has published all but one significant manuscript. Each has been edited by a different person with mixed results, creating one of the most productive posthumous literary lives on record.

A Moveable Feast. New York: Charles Scribner's Sons, 1964. Largely edited by Mary Hemingway, who withheld two chapters and rearranged the sequence of others, this is the memoir of Hemingway's early days in Paris. Loosely chronological, the chapters conflate the 1922–1926 period of Hemingway's life into a series of encounters with Paris life and the literary gathering there. Gertrude Stein, the Fitzgeralds, and Ford Madox Ford all appear foolish compared to the young Hemingway and his wife, Hadley.

By-Line: Ernest Hemingway. Edited by William White. New York: Charles Scribner's Sons, 1967. A sampling of Hemingway's journalism and essays, including generous reprints from the 1922–1923 *Toronto Star*, the *Esquire* essays from the 1930s, the North American News Alliance dispatches from the Spanish Civil War (1937–1938), the *PM* newspaper stories from the Chinese front (1941), and his *Collier's* magazine essays from World War II (1944), as well as other essays.

Islands in the Stream. New York: Charles Scribner's Sons, 1970. This three-part novel, silently edited by Hemingway's first biographer, Carlos Baker, grew out of the Bimini novel begun in 1945 and was much revised in Hemingway's lifetime. Once it was to be part of a land-sea-air trilogy about World War II, but that plan was abandoned. The first section introduces the painter, Thomas Hudson, and his prewar life on Bimini; the second section leaps forward to the war years when Hudson is ashore in Cuba between submarine patrols; the final part, "At Sea," details Hudson's last patrol, during which he is seriously, perhaps fatally, wounded while pursuing German sailors.

Ernest Hemingway, Cub Reporter. Edited by Matthew J. Bruccoli. University of Pittsburgh Press, 1970. Twelve stories Hemingway wrote for

The Kansas City Star (1917–1918), and several stories possibly written by Hemingway.

Ernest Hemingway's Apprenticeship: Oak Park, 1916–1917. Edited by Matthew J. Bruccoli. Washington, D.C.: NCR Microcard Editions, 1971. Thirty-nine newspaper pieces, three short stories, four poems, and the senior class prophecy written by Hemingway while at Oak Park and River Forest High School.

The Nick Adams Stories. Edited by Philip Young. New York: Charles Scribner's Sons, 1972. A chronologically arranged collection of all the Hemingway stories featuring the character Nick Adams. Included are previously unpublished stories and fragments, some of which are not included in the *Complete Short Stories* described below.

Ernest Hemingway: 88 Poems. Edited by Nicholas Gerogiannis. New York: Harcourt Brace Jovanovich/Bruccoli Clark, 1979. Includes all of his published poetry from high school and the Paris years, and collects his unpublished poetry that remained in manuscript.

Ernest Hemingway: Selected Letters 1917–1961. Edited by Carlos Baker. New York: Charles Scribner's Sons, 1981.

Dateline: Toronto. Edited by William White. New York: Charles Scribner's Sons, 1985. The "complete edition" of Hemingway's *Toronto Star* journalism, 1920–1924. Of the 172 news stories and features, more than half were written in Europe from 1922 to 1923.

The Dangerous Summer. Introduction by James A. Michener. New York: Charles Scribner's Sons, 1985. Silently edited by Scribner editor Michael Pietsch, this nonfiction book follows the 1959 Spanish summer when Antonio Ordóñez and Luis Miguel Dominguín fought a series of *mano-a-mano* (competitive) bullfights up and down the Iberian Peninsula.

The Garden of Eden. New York: Charles Scribner's Sons, 1986. Hemingway's unfinished 1920s novel set in Provence, edited not so silently by Tom Jenks. This complex manuscript originally included two parallel sets of complementary characters, both sets muddled by sexual conflicts and erotic experiments. The published version eliminated one set, leaving David Bourne, a writer, married to a destructive wife, Catherine, who brings a second woman, Maria, into their lives. The novel is part of Hemingway's post–World War II effort to depict the condition of the twentieth-century artist.

The Complete Short Stories of Ernest Hemingway. New York: Charles Scribner's Sons, 1987. Subtitled the Finca Vigía Edition, this collection republished all the stories printed during Hemingway's life and several that remained unpublished at his death, including a section he cut out of the Bimini novel and two chapters from a still-unpublished manuscript he put aside in 1928.

The Only Thing That Counts: The Ernest Hemingway/Maxwell Perkins Correspondence, 1925–1947. Edited by Matthew J. Bruccoli. New York: Scribners, 1996. The complete correspondence between Hemingway and his editor at Scribners, one of the most significant literary correspondences of this century.

True at First Light. Edited by Patrick Hemingway. New York: Scribner, 1999. This "fictional memoir," set on an African safari, was begun in 1954 and left unfinished at Hemingway's death. Edited by his son, Patrick Hemingway, the book is an amalgam of genres. Part of it is a safari story told by the narrator, Papa, who leads the reader through the killing of Mary's lion and his leopard. But much of the book mixes memory with desire in both comic and serious meditations on religion, marriage, and the narrator's early life. The book is also a contemplation on how to live after the fall from grace, how to live in Eden in its fallen state, a theme obvious here and present in Hemingway's work since "Big Two-Hearted River," written in 1924.

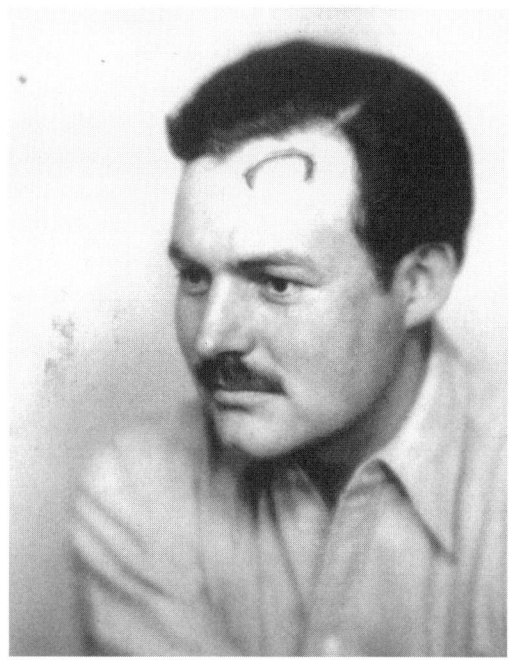

Publicity photo of Hemingway, Paris, March 1928. With the publication of *The Sun Also Rises* in 1926, Hemingway graduated from being a Left Bank cult writer appearing in small literary magazines to a promising young novelist with a distinguished New York publisher. The still-raw scar on his forehead is from a falling bathroom skylight; an emergency-room doctor hurriedly stitched it closed in the middle of the night.

CRITICAL RECEPTION

EARLY ADULATION: 1925–1929: If ever a writer was at one with his era, it was Ernest Hemingway at the beginning of his career. Between the publication of *In Our Time* in 1925 and *A Farewell to Arms* in 1929, he gathered little but praise from the New York critics, for whom he epitomized the American expatriate writer, the Left Bank bohemian. When *The Sun Also Rises* appeared in 1926, the *Chicago Tribune* did not care for its characters or its attitudes, but in New York, where literary opinion made or broke a writer's career, the critics raved about the novel. The dialogue was brilliant, direct, uncluttered, completely free of sentiment. Phrases such as "lean, hard, athletic, clean, and masculine" were used to describe Hemingway's diction. Conrad Aiken thought Hemingway was "the most exciting of contemporary American writers of fiction" (*New York Herald Tribune,* 31 October 1926). Burton Rascoe said that the dialogue of the novel was "so natural that it hardly seems written at all—one hears it" (*New York Sun,* 6 November 1926). Herbert Gorman praised the "sense of cool repression . . . Not once does the author intervene" (*The New York World,* 14 November 1926).

Those not won over by *The Sun Also Rises* were swept away by *A Farewell to Arms,* Hemingway's first best-selling book. Published in September, the 31,050 copies of the first Scribners edition sold out so fast that two more printings were required before the end of the month, and within the first year 79,251 copies were sold. Understated, laconic, and detached, the novel spoke to America's disgust with the Great European War, its appetite for sad love stories, and its growing isolationist attitudes. The same Chicago reviewer who thought *The Sun Also Rises* a disgrace now called Hemingway a genius. *Time* magazine joined the mainstream, allowing that Hemingway had fulfilled the promise his early reviewers had seen. The first-line New York critics praised the novel lavishly: more dramatic than *The Sun Also Rises,* more romantic in the best sense, more poetic. Hemingway's description of the Caporetto retreat was recognized by almost every reviewer as a classic narrative. The major debate centered on genre: was this a love story set in the war, or a war story with a backdrop of romance?

Along with their praise, the national reviewers now began holding Hemingway to a higher standard. Here was no one-book author, no flash in the pan, but a writer whom many were calling the spokesman for their generation. As a result, more attention was paid to his experiments with voice and style, to his ability to create characters, and to his literary forebears: Stendhal, Rudyard Kipling, and Stephen Crane. With a backlog of two novels and two collections of short stories, the critics had no trouble categorizing Hemingway's themes (the effects of violence, the inevitability of loss, the failure of traditional values) and analyzing the effects of Hemingway's detachment that forced the reader to reach his own conclusions. Tags such as "un-literary" and "non-intellectual" were applied to him as positive attributes.

BACKLASH OF THE 1930S: With the stock-market crash of 1929 that signaled the end of the Jazz Age, America sank into the Great Depression, during which time much of the fiction of the 1920s was repudiated for its nihilistic characters who thought only of themselves and nothing about the greater good of the group. This tidal turn brought several now-forgotten proletariat writers to national attention, and left at least one masterpiece, John Steinbeck's *The Grapes of Wrath* (1939). Just when the critics thought they had Hemingway neatly pegged, he confused them by not writing another novel for eight years. His next three published works were a nonfiction book on bullfighting (*Death in the Afternoon*, 1932), a collection of stories (*Winner Take Nothing*, 1934) and a nonfiction safari book (*Green Hills of Africa*, 1935), all of which got mixed reviews.

While Hemingway's defenders found much positive to say about *Death in the Afternoon*, its complexity gave almost every reviewer something to complain about: it was not a novel; it had no narrative structure; the sentences were too long. R. L. Duffus in *The New York Times* (25 September 1932) said that "the famous Hemingway style is neither so clear nor so forceful" as in his fiction. Granville Hicks, in *The Nation* (9 November 1932), thought the book would be largely ignored had it not been written by Hemingway. Max Eastman in *The New Republic* (7 June 1933) said the book was "filled with juvenile romantic sentimentalizing over a rather lamentable practice of the culture of Spain."

Winner Take Nothing fared not much better. Despite such now-classic stories as "A Clean, Well-Lighted Place" and "Fathers and Sons," the critics were largely bored: here was nothing new. Clifton Fadiman in *The New Yorker* (28 October 1933) found the stories "unsatisfactory" with "strong echoes of earlier work." In the *Saturday Review of Literature* (28 October 1933), Horace Gregory called the stories "studies of brutality, cold lust, and pathetic demoralization," all very Kiplingesque. The *New York Herald Tribune* allowed that Hemingway's prose "always reaches certain levels of excellence," that his art was "deliberate," but "the hard, bright surface has been made to cover much hollow thinking and sloppy emotion."

By the time *Green Hills of Africa* appeared in 1935, 25 percent of the American workforce was without work. Cardboard and tin "Hoovervilles," filled with broken men and hungry children, haunted the edge of many towns. Factories closed while the rich retreated into their money. Photographs of weary men standing in soup lines were inescapable. It was little wonder that a nonfiction account of an expensive safari would seem to be conspicuous consumption. "An overextended book about hunting, with a few incidental felicities," said John Chamberlain in *The New York Times* (25 October 1935). In the *Saturday Review of Literature* (26 October 1935), Bernard DeVoto found that "being bored by Ernest

"It is dangerous to use the terms 'great' and 'masterpiece' about any contemporary book. The literary reviews of thirty years ago are funnier than the women's hats of that vintage. But I shall not much care if thirty years from now it seem ridiculous to have agreed noisily to that FOR WHOM THE BELL TOLLS is indeed that most unusual and most desirable luxury, a great love story."

Sinclair Lewis

From the Introduction to *For Whom the Bell Tolls* (Princeton: Printed for the Members of the Limited Editions Club by the Princeton University Press, 1942).

Hemingway is a new experience. . . . An unimportant book. A pretty small book for a big man to write." Granville Hicks in *New Masses* (19 November 1935) found "perhaps ten pages that are interesting . . . the rest of the book is just plain dull. . . . I should like to have Hemingway write a novel about a strike. . . . In six years Hemingway has not produced a book even remotely worthy of his talents."

Hicks and other left-wing critics wanted Hemingway to become a proletarian novelist writing about the troubles of the underclass, but when the author produced his semiproletariat novel *To Have and Have Not* (1937), its violence, sexuality, and rough language disturbed many reviewers. Some called it confused, transitional, or weak. "An empty book," said Donald Adams in *The New York Times* (17 October 1937). "A more serious Hemingway," countered *Time* magazine. Fortunately for Hemingway, he was not dependent upon reviewers, for his reputation and public image guaranteed substantial sales of any book he published. Between 1933 and 1936, Hemingway's semiregular essays in *Esquire* magazine had created a nationwide audience that bought 36,000 copies of his new novel in the first five months of its publication and put it among the top ten best-sellers for three months.

THE 1940S: TRIUMPH, SILENCE, AND CRITICAL BOMBARDMENT: By 1939, critical opinion was of two schools: either Hemingway was in transition to a new phase with his 1930s experiments, or he was a voice from the past with nothing new to say. In 1940, the publication of *For Whom the Bell Tolls* put such critical opinion to rest as Hemingway's novel of the Spanish Civil War became an enormous best-seller. Published on 21 October, the first printing of 75,000 copies sold out immediately. By the end of December, 189,000 copies had been sold. Four months later the total was almost 500,000 copies. In *The New Republic* Edmund Wilson wrote, "Hemingway the artist is with us again; and it is like having an old friend back" (28 October 1940). Nearly every major review was in agreement. In the *New York Herald Tribune,* John Chamberlain declared that *For Whom the Bell Tolls* "redeems a decade of futility" (20 October 1940). Donald Adams said in *The New York Times* that it was "the best book

Ernest Hemingway has written, the fullest, the deepest, the truest" (20 October 1940). In *The Nation*, Margaret Marshall found the novel setting "a new standard for Hemingway in characterization, dialogue, suspense, and compassion" (26 October 1940). "Gone is the self conscious 'little Hemingway,'" declared Howard Mumford Jones in the *Saturday Review of Literature*. "Gone is the Hemingway manner. Manner has been replaced by style" (26 October 1940).

During World War II, Hemingway wrote no new fiction, edited a collection of war stories, and contributed feature journalism to *Collier's* magazine. In 1950, after a ten-year silence, he published *Across the River and Into the Trees*, about which critics found little good to say. His staunchest defenders, such as Charles Poore, had to acknowledge that the novel was "heavily weighted with the foolishness of grandeur" (*The New York Times,* 7 September 1950). Joe Jackson in the *San Francisco Chronicle* called it "a parody of Hemingway at his best" (7 September 1950). "An unfortunate novel and unpleasant for anyone to review who respects Hemingway's talent," wrote Maxwell Geismar in the *Saturday Review of Literature* (9 September 1950). "It is not only Hemingway's worst novel," Geismar said, "it is a synthesis of everything that is bad in his previous work." Despite such reviews, the 75,000-copy first printing of *Across the River and into the Trees* sold out quickly, and the novel was on the best-seller list for twenty-one weeks.

THE 1950S: NOBEL LAUREATE: Hard on the heels of the critical bashing of *Across the River and into the Trees* came Hemingway's response: *The Old Man and the Sea*. First published in 1952 in a single issue of *Life* magazine, which sold out five million copies within a week, the story of the old fisherman and his giant marlin was a Book-of-the-Month Club selection and a national best-seller for twenty-six weeks. Hemingway's national and international reputation reached new heights. Before the year was out, the novel was translated into Chinese, Danish, Dutch, Finnish, French, German, Italian, Norwegian, and Swedish. In 1953 Hemingway was awarded the Pulitzer Prize in literature for *The Old Man and the Sea,* followed by the Nobel Prize in literature in 1954.

After the publication of *The Old Man and the Sea,* no new Hemingway books were published before his death in 1961. During this period, he wrote prodigiously, leaving behind in various stages of completion three novels, one memoir, and another book on bullfighting. While he kept to his solitary work in Cuba, three American academics published groundbreaking books which determined the course of Hem-

Key West, Florida, April 1928. Clarence Hemingway observes his son Ernest standing beside his new Model A Ford. Dr. Hemingway and Grace had been on a cruise to Havana, celebrating his fifty-seventh birthday. In Ernest and Pauline's rented Key West house, the manuscript of *A Farewell to Arms* had reached 108 pages. Eight months after this photograph was taken, Clarence Hemingway put a pistol to his temple and killed himself.

ingway studies for more than twenty years. The first to appear was Carlos Baker's *Hemingway: The Writer as Artist* (Princeton: Princeton University Press, 1952), a seminal work which examined each of Hemingway's books, describing its artistry, technique, structure, and latent symbolism. Baker saw that Hemingway was far better read than most recognized, that he was a conscious craftsman, and that Hemingway's "iceberg theory" of writing left seven-eighths of the story frequently below the waterline. Once the reader became aware of this technique, Baker said "he is likely to find symbols operating everywhere" in Hemingway's texts. Baker's reading of Hemingway presented a more complex and deliberate author than previously seen, a writer who deserved the same close reading reserved for the Metaphysical Poets. That same year, Philip Young's influential *Ernest Hemingway* (New York: Rinehart, 1952) drew connections between Hemingway and Mark Twain, and established the "Hemingway Code" and the "code hero" from whom the "Hemingway hero" learns to act "with grace under pressure."[1] The bearer of the "code" instructs the "hero" in matters of "honor and courage which in a life of tension and pain make a man a man." Young's equally important contribution was to bring into focus the effects of violence in Hemingway's texts, drawing the connection between Hemingway's own wounding and the recurring wounded men in his fiction.

Between Baker and Young there developed the belief that the "Hemingway hero" was essentially the same man from one work to another. This approach to Hemingway's fiction was given more credence by Charles Fenton's *The Apprenticeship of Ernest Hemingway* (New York: Farrar, Straus & Young, 1954), which provided biographical information on Hemingway's childhood in Oak Park, his wounding as a Red Cross man in Italy, and his newspaper work in Kansas City, Toronto, and Europe. While doing so, Fenton drew obvious parallels between Heming-

way's life and his fiction. Thus, in a three-year period, Baker, Fenton, and Young laid down the major critical concepts that governed Hemingway studies for the postwar generation of scholars and critics.

The last major critical contribution of the 1950s was George Plimpton's long and informative interview with Hemingway that appeared in *The Paris Review* in the Spring 1958 issue. Because Hemingway's keen sense of literary history taught him the value of an author manipulating the future's assessment of his work in advance, he insisted that he write out the answers to Plimpton's questions, and in some cases he reconfigured the question to his own focus. The resulting interview completed the portrait of the artist for the 1950s generation. Hemingway confirmed that he was a deliberate writer who composed slowly and revised extensively. As much as he regretted Philip Young's thesis about the effects of his Italian wounding, he allowed that the "effects of wounds vary greatly . . . sometimes give confidence." He spoke of learning from numerous dead authors (Gustave Flaubert, Stendhal, Leo Tolstoy, John Donne, Andrew Marvell, and Dante) and painters (Tintoretto, Hieronymus Bosch, Pieter Brueghel, Francisco Goya, Giotto, Paul Cézanne, and Vincent Van Gogh). And he restated his "iceberg theory" of writing: "Anything you can omit that you know you still have in the writing and its quality will show." As for symbols, yes, they were probably there, but he would prefer not to explain his own work. The greatest gift for a writer, he said, was "a built-in, shock-proof shit detector" which was the "writer's radar."

POSTHUMOUS HEMINGWAY: Following Hemingway's death in 1961, several significant critical studies appeared that consolidated, extended, and to some degree exhausted the work from the 1950s. Particularly influential was Earl Rovit's *Ernest Hemingway* (New York: Twayne, 1963), which reconfigured the code hero/Hemingway hero concept into the less confusing relationship between the "tutor" and the "tyro." Joseph DeFalco's *The Hero in Hemingway's Short Stories* (Pittsburgh: University of Pittsburgh Press, 1963) was both a psychoanalytical study and an examination of the relationship between structure and theme in the stories. Robert W. Lewis, in *Hemingway on Love* (Austin: University of Texas

FROM A REVIEW OF
ISLANDS IN THE STREAM

"The new generations, my impression is, want to abolish both war and love, not love as a physical act but love as a religion, a creed to help us suffer better. The sacred necessity of suffering no longer seems sacred or necessary, and Hemingway speaks across the Sixties as strangely as a medieval saint; I suspect few readers younger than myself could believe, from this sad broken testament, how we *did* love Hemingway and, after pity feels merely impudent, love him still."

John Updike

From "Papa's Sad Testament," *New Statesman*, 80 (16 October 1970): 489.

Press, 1965), made a thorough examination of the function of love in Hemingway's major texts. Constance Montgomery's *Hemingway in Michigan* (New York: Fleet, 1966) provided biographical details on Hemingway's summers at and around Walloon Lake from 1900 to 1921, including parallels between his short stories and real characters and settings. Robert O. Stephens's *Hemingway's Nonfiction* (Chapel Hill: University of North Carolina Press, 1968) was the first and best analysis of the journalism and essays and the first study of the relationships between Hemingway's nonfiction and fiction. Delbert Wylder's *Hemingway's Heroes* (Albuquerque: University of New Mexico Press, 1969) broke away from the single-hero theory to show the uniqueness of each Hemingway hero. Jackson Benson's *Hemingway: The Writer's Art of Self Defense* (Minneapolis: University of Minnesota Press, 1969) was a revisionist reading of the major texts, and Jackson Bryer edited *Fifteen Modern American Authors* (Durham, N.C.: Duke University Press, 1969), a survey of research and criticism that gave scholars a starting point in Hemingway studies.

The 1960s also produced the first wave of biographies and memoirs written by survivors. From inside the family came sister Marcelline Hemingway Sanford's *At the Hemingways* (Boston: Little, Brown, 1962) and younger brother Leicester Hemingway's *My Brother, Ernest Hemingway* (Cleveland: World, 1962). Anyone who knew Hemingway during his Paris years was certain to mention him in his or her memoirs, including Sylvia Beach's *Shakespeare and Company* (New York: Harcourt, Brace, 1959). Morley Callaghan's *That Summer in Paris* (New York: Coward-McCann, 1963) and Robert McAlmon's *McAlmon and the Lost Generation* (Lincoln: University of Nebraska Press, 1962) provided a spate of biographical information encouraging readers to correlate Hemingway's life with his fiction. This practice quickly inverted itself when scholars began filling in blank spots in the biography with the fiction, a fallacy called the "biographical trap." The 1960s were capped by Carlos Baker's *Ernest Hemingway: A Life Story* (New York: Scribners, 1969), which remains the best single-volume biography.

The 1970s brought about a significant shift in Hemingway studies, largely due to the opening of the massive Hemingway collection of manuscripts and letters housed at the John F. Kennedy Library in Boston. With exceptions of the *Death in the Afternoon* manuscript at the University of Texas at Austin and the *Green Hills of Africa* manuscript at the University of Virginia, all of the major and most of the minor first drafts of Hemingway's novels and short stories are at the Kennedy Library. The opening of this trove began the first serious studies of the author at work. In 1973 Sheldon Grebstein's excellent study *Hemingway's Craft* (Carbondale: Southern Illinois University Press) called attention to the manuscripts of *For Whom the Bell Tolls* and *A Farewell to Arms,* then temporarily housed in Harvard's Houghton Library. In 1976, Michael Reynolds's *Hemingway's First War* (Princeton: Princeton University Press) studied the creation of *A Farewell to Arms,* including several excised, revised, or rearranged passages from the manuscript. Frederic Svoboda followed with *Hemingway & The Sun Also Rises* (Lawrence: University Press of Kansas, 1983), a detailed analysis of that novel's first draft and its revisions. Susan Beegel's manuscript study *Hemingway's Craft of Omission* (Ann Arbor, Mich.: UMI Research Press, 1988) gave an intelligent, balanced analysis of what Hemingway left out of four texts: "Fifty Grand," "A Natural History of the Dead," *Death in the Afternoon,* and "After the Storm." In 1989, Paul Smith published *A Reader's Guide to the Short Stories of Ernest Hemingway* (Boston: G. K. Hall), in which he examined all extant manuscripts, reaching persuasive conclusions on the composition history of the stories. In 1991 Jacqueline Tavernier-Courbin published *Ernest Hemingway's A Moveable Feast* (Boston: Northeastern University Press), which among other things fully described the manuscript of the book, the changes wrought by Hemingway and those made by his executors. These studies and others like them combined to form a much clearer picture of the writer at work: his method of composition, his revisions, and his drafts.

By the 1980s and into the 1990s, the availability of Hemingway manuscripts and letters, along with new research tools, made several new biographies possible. In 1981 two bibliographic volumes on Hemingway's reading were published—James Brasch and Joseph Sigman's *Hemingway's Library* (New York: Garland) and Michael Reynolds's *Hemingway's Reading 1910–1940* (Princeton: Princeton University Press). There followed mass-market biographies by Jeffrey Meyers, Kenneth Lynn, Peter Griffin, James Mellow, and Michael Reynolds. Although based on many of the same primary documents, each biography had its own view of Hemingway the man and the writer. The new biographies and the manuscripts of the posthumously published novels came together in Robert Fleming's excellent study *The Face in the Mirror: Hemingway's Writers* (Tuscaloosa: University of Alabama Press, 1994).

As the sometimes-controversial posthumous Hemingway books were published, his literary estate opened the once-closed manuscripts to scholars, who in turn produced a spate of revisionist Hemingway studies. *The Garden of Eden,* with its sexual role-playing, forced serious revaluation of what Hemingway was writing in the postwar years; combined with the rise of gender theory, the impact of *The Garden of Eden* studies prompted revisionist studies of all of Hemingway. First in scholarly journals and then in several books, Hemingway gender studies have encouraged readers to consider all of Hemingway's writing, not merely a few privileged works. Mark Spilka's *Hemingway's Quarrel With Androgyny* (Lincoln: University of Nebraska Press, 1990) was followed by Nancy Comley and Robert Scholes's *Hemingway's Genders* (New Haven: Yale University Press, 1994), Rose Marie Burwell's *Hemingway: The Postwar Years and the Posthumous Novels* (New York: Cambridge University Press, 1996), and Debra Moddelmog's *Reading Desire: In Pursuit of Ernest Hemingway* (Ithaca, N.Y.: Cornell University Press, 1999).

ART IMITATING LIFE

Probably no other American author's life has been so closely associated with his fiction as has Ernest Hemingway's. This correlation on the part of readers has produced several misleading conclusions, the most erroneous of which is the widely held belief that Hemingway first lived an experience and then re-created it in fiction, that his fiction is thinly veiled autobiography. In fact, his fiction is almost never unvarnished biography, and to read it as such will produce a Hemingway who never existed. With that caveat in mind, one may still recognize the many parallels between the life and the fiction, parallels whose significance must rest with the fiction, not the life of the author.

The short stories, particularly those with Nick Adams as the central character, provide a strong temptation to be read as coming directly from life. Like Nick, Ernest spent his summers in a family cottage beside a northern Michigan lake. Both author and character have a doctor for a father, a dominant woman for a mother, and more than one sister as siblings. Both Ernest and Nick prefer the outdoor life of trout fishing to the confining strictures of home and family. Both at one time are involved with a girl named Marge. Both boys have friends who are Ojibway Indians, and both run afoul of a game warden because of an out-of-season

Africa, 1934. Ernest, Pauline, and their Key West friend Charles Thompson spent two months on an East African safari that fulfilled Hemingway's boyhood dream of hunting on the same grounds popularized by Theodore Roosevelt's 1909 safari. Here Hemingway is pictured at the end of the hunt, considerably trimmed down from a bout with dysentery, holding up two kudu trophies.

kill. Both go to World War I, where they suffer serious wounds. Most importantly, perhaps, both Ernest and his character Nick Adams want to become writers. With so many close parallels, it takes a determined mind to remember that art is never life itself, not even the art of Hemingway.

For example, Hemingway's father, Dr. Clarence Hemingway, did sometimes minister to the local Ojibway Indians living close to the family cottage on Walloon Lake, but he never performed a cesarean delivery with a jackknife as scalpel on an Indian woman, as Dr. Adams does in "Indian Camp." And although Ernest once had a relationship with Marjorie Bump, he broke up with her by mail, not beside the lake at night as Nick Adams does in "The End of Something." Every Hemingway biographer to his or her regret has given in to the temptation to take some detail from the fiction as accurate biography. For example, Hemingway claimed in a letter to F. Scott Fitzgerald that he wrote the story "Out of Season" immediately after the events described in it happened to himself and Hadley at Cortina, Italy. In the story the husband and wife, who have been arguing, are following a local guide to fish illegally before the season opens. In the course of the story the reader becomes aware that "out of season" applies equally well to the couple's marital relationship. Many biographers have assumed that the fishing season at Cortina was closed when Ernest returned there to meet Hadley in April of 1923. In fact, as Italian documents from the period verify, the fishing season had already opened, but for the impact of the story it was more effective to have it closed. Be warned: Hemingway always changed factual experience or invented details to meet the needs of his fiction.

The story is never his life, but the *writing* of the story may tell something about his life at that moment he wrote it. For example, "Big Two-Hearted River" is not the biography of Hemingway returning from the war in Italy. Ernest and two friends did fish the Fox River that summer of 1919, but their outing bore little resemblance to Nick Adams's solitary camping trip. The first aborted draft of the story begins with three characters, one of them still limping from a war wound, getting off the train at Seney. In the second draft, Nick is alone getting off the train, and the limp is removed. The war is there beneath the surface of the story and beneath the surface of Nick's mind. What the story does not tell us is how Ernest Hemingway felt that summer of 1919 on the Fox River. If the story has biographical significance, its import must focus on the summer of 1924 when Hemingway wrote the story in Paris, a long way from upper Michigan. The original ending of the story, published posthumously as "On Writing," comes closer to being biographic than the story as published.[2]

Hemingway himself is to blame for much of the biographical reading of his texts, for *The Sun Also Rises*, the work that brought him to public attention, was and remains a roman à clef, in which almost every character has a real and once-readily identifiable counterpart. In the novel, Hemingway conflates the experiences of two summers in Spain (1924 and 1925) when he and friends stayed at Burguete, fished for trout, and attended the feria of San Fermín at Pamplona. In the novel, Brett Ashley is the Circe figure whose attractiveness makes the men behave badly. Engaged to Mike Campbell while having a brief affair with Robert Cohn, she leaves them both for an affair with the young bullfighter, Pedro Romero. That summer of 1925, Lady Duff Twysden, engaged to Pat Guthrie, was having a brief affair with Harold Loeb. All three joined Ernest and Hadley for the Pamplona feria. Ernest was possessive of Duff; Harold resented it; Pat stayed drunk; and Duff did not run off with the young bullfighter, Niño de la Palma. Given the gossip of the Left Bank, the prototypes for Hemingway's characters became common knowledge.[3] Three generations later, no one particularly cares who was who in the novel, but one understands how Hemingway's early reputation was established as a writer who used his friends and enemies in his work. He was perfectly capable of using a sometime American poet, Chard Powers Smith, as the character Hubert Elliot in "Mr. and Mrs. Elliot," using the style of Gertrude Stein to satirize a type of dilettante all too present on the Left Bank of Paris during the 1920s. No one remembers Smith, but the story remains a classic of its kind.

Hemingway's second novel, *A Farewell to Arms,* was equal parts invention and firsthand experience, but it took almost fifty years before anyone was able to differentiate the two parts.[4] Until then it was widely assumed that the experience of Frederic Henry on the Italian front was largely the same as Hemingway's experience. Both author and character were volunteers, driving ambulances in Italy. Both were wounded by mortar shells; both recuperated in the Red Cross hospital in Milan; and both fell in love with a Red Cross nurse. However, Frederic's experience takes place between 1915 and 1917, while Hemingway did not arrive in Italy until 1918. Frederic is wounded in the mountains at Plava in the spring of 1917; Hemingway was wounded on the Venetian plain at Fossalta in 1918. The Caporetto retreat, which is at the heart of the novel, took place in October 1917, when Hemingway was working in Kansas City. The battles referred to in the novel all took place before Hemingway left Kansas City. In 1917 there was no Red Cross hospital in Milan, but there was in 1918. Hemingway did fall in love with Agnes Von Kurowsky, his nurse, but she never became pregnant; he did not desert the Italian army; and they did not flee to Switzerland. Using what Hemingway learned and experienced in Italy, the novel is anchored in realistic detail, both historical and topographical, that the author did not experience firsthand, details so accurate that Italian critics who took part in the retreat from Caporetto were certain that Hemingway must have been there. This ability to use firsthand experiences and secondhand material with equal dexterity characterized Hemingway's earliest mature writing. Of the eighteen vignettes from *in our time,* at least half were based on secondhand sources, but it is virtually impossible to differentiate them from those based on Hemingway's own experiences.

Novelist Lee Smith has said that an author gets his or her first two novels free, that is, they come out of life experiences. After that, she said, one relies on the lives of one's friends: a truism which more than one friend of a writer has come to know and regret. With *The Sun Also*

Rises and *A Farewell to Arms,* Hemingway had used up the Left Bank of Paris, the feria of Pamplona, and World War I as material for novels. Unlike almost every other American writer, he refused, early and late in his career, to write about his home life in Oak Park. He gave it a "miss," he said, asking what sort of a man would want to bomb his own hometown.

Even when writing *Green Hills of Africa,* purported to be "an absolutely true book," Hemingway knew that life is messy and art should not be. Although the incidents related in this safari book all actually happened, a good deal was left out, and the remainder was rearranged wherever the structure necessitated. Pauline Hemingway's unpublished safari journal reveals the difference between reality and Hemingway's art.[5] *Green Hills of Africa,* which is as much about aesthetics and writing as about hunting, is narrated by Hemingway, the author, observing himself as character. If that character sometimes appears vain, selfish, or a braggart, the reader must remember that Hemingway, the author, created him that way. In fact, one should never forget that Hemingway, as their creator, is all of his characters, strong and weak, male and female.

To Have and Have Not and *For Whom the Bell Tolls* take place in settings which Hemingway knew from experience, but the action of each novel is largely imaginary. *To Have and Have Not* is set in Key West, Havana, and the Gulf Stream—locales which Hemingway explored intensively between 1930 and 1936. Having fished for marlin out of Havana for several summers, Hemingway knew the setting intimately, and with his avid interest in revolutions, he understood the Cuban politics that eventually result in the death of Harry Morgan. His friend Josie Russell told Ernest enough stories about prohibition rumrunners to add to Morgan's character, just as Hemingway's Key West lawyer served as a model for the fictional lawyer "Bee-lips." The drunken vets turning the barroom floor sloppy with blood were also well-known features of Key West. Several other of Hemingway's acquaintances served as character models for the novel, affirming Ernest's own warning that it was usually a mistake to know an author well.

For Whom the Bell Tolls was built on settings, scenes, and incidents which Hemingway knew from observing them as a journalist during the Spanish Civil War. He knew by heart the siege of Madrid, the streets, the bars, and the restaurants. He knew the Guadarrama Mountains from before and during the war. The bridge that Robert Jordan must destroy lies below La Granja and can be easily found on any good map. But it was a solid stone bridge, not one of steel girders as in the novel. Hemingway knew the real bridge, had walked across it, and knew that it would take more dynamite than a man could carry on his back to bring it down. So he changed the bridge to steel. Robert Jordan was invented from Hemingway's chance acquaintance with Robert Merriman, an American who died during the war, and from T. E. Lawrence's adventures as Lawrence of Arabia during World War I. None of the action of the novel was ever experienced by Hemingway. The band of partisans is composed of character types whom he knew well from his long experience of traveling in Spain. The settings, climate, terrain, and central conflict of the novel all came directly from firsthand experience, but the characters and their mission to destroy the bridge were Hemingway's creation.

Across the River and into the Trees is another novel in which the setting is map-accurate, the time and terrain well known to Hemingway, and the characters half invented and half based on experience. After his 1948 visit to Venice when he met his young muse, Adriana Ivancich, Hemingway invented the last three days of Colonel Richard Cantwell's life, during which his bitter experience of military politics is gradually expiated by the love of the young Venetian beauty, Renata. Cantwell is largely based on Hemingway's lifelong desire to be a field commander, his considerable reading about the art of war, his close observations of the battle of Hürtgenwald, and his much-admired friend, Colonel Charles "Buck" Lanham, who led the military life that Hemingway envied. The novel is about the war with the war left out; we have only the colonel's commentary on the action, in many ways not unlike Dante's commentary on Italian politics in the *Inferno*. Cantwell says at one point that he sometimes is Mr. Dante. Any student who wishes to explore the levels of this novel would do well to read the *Inferno* along with a detailed commentary on it.

The last of his books published during Hemingway's lifetime was the novella *The Old Man and the Sea,* which continues the pattern of creating an imaginary character engaged in an activity, in this case marlin fishing on the Gulf Stream, which Hemingway knew better than any writer alive. Santiago fishes out of Cojimar, the same village at which Hemingway docked his boat, the *Pilar.* Several different Cubans have vied for the honor of being the model for Santiago, but he remains Hemingway's creation. Based on an experience from the 1930s when Hemingway found a Cuban fisherman far out in the Gulf Stream with the shark-ravaged remains of a huge marlin strapped to the side of his boat, the novel's seeming simplicity, its allegorical overtones, and the absence of sexuality made it hugely popular worldwide.

Hemingway's posthumously published works are problematic for the reader who does not have the author's final version, but all of them are more autobiographical than his earlier work. *A Moveable Feast* is a semifictionalized memoir of Hemingway's early years in Paris. The characters—Gertrude Stein, Ford Madox Ford, Sylvia Beach, F. Scott and Zelda Fitzgerald—are all drawn from life but drawn by a writer getting in the last word. Ernest and his wife Hadley observe the scene with an innocence they probably lacked at the time. *The Dangerous Summer* is a nonfictional but deeply personal account of the 1959 bullfights in Spain, with commentary on the food, terrain, and politics of the corrida. *Islands in the Stream* is thinly veiled fiction based on Hemingway's summers in the 1930s fishing from Bimini and his submarine-patrol activities out of Cuba from 1942 to 1943. The central character is a painter, but his values, his family, and his personal problems resemble those of the author. The most fictional part is the last section, the pursuit of the German submariners, which never happened. *True at First Light,* based on Hemingway's 1953 African safari, is filled with specific detail, using real people whose names were not changed in the unfinished draft. But much of the action is fictional, imagined on the basis of what Hemingway had experienced. The most complex posthumous book—*The Garden of Eden*—is also the most severely edited. Almost half of the novel Hemingway wrote was eliminated from the published version. It is set on terrain that Hemingway knew from his second marriage and had revisited several times in the 1950s. The characters are composites of people known and imagined. To read the novel as biography would be a mistake. All of the posthumous books are, in different ways, concerned with the writer or artist and his craft. In this sense, they are early postmodernism: the writer writing about the writer writing.

HEMINGWAY'S LASTING IMPACT ON AMERICAN FICTION

Hemingway is one of the few authors to begin writing fiction in the modernist era who continued to be influential into the postmodernist era. His impact on American fiction has been and continues to be pervasive. Growing up as he did on nineteenth-century authors, Hemingway's first and most important development was finding a voice for his century. One need only place a page from Henry James next to one of Hemingway's to understand the difference between the old and the new. James speaks to the reader in a voice no longer familiar: decorous, educated, subtle, and sensitive; Hemingway's voice, his rhythms and diction, are as familiar as the closest movie screen. Like Twain, like Faulkner, Hemingway captured and refined an American voice for his time. When Nick Adams and Marjorie watch the moon rising over the lake in "The End of

Something," their conversation is classic Americana. Marjorie asks him what is bothering him. Nick replies:

> "I don't know."
>
> "Of course you know."
>
> "No I don't."
>
> "Go on and say it."
>
> Nick looked on at the moon, coming up over the hills.
>
> "It isn't fun any more."
>
> He was afraid to look at Marjorie. Then he looked at her. She sat there with her back toward him. He looked at her back. "It isn't fun any more. Not any of it."[6]

Hemingway wrote that scene in 1924. It could have been written yesterday.

In many Hemingway stories, his readers must become participants, or his narrative loses its impact. Before Hemingway wrote, the author not only told what was happening but also explained what to think about it, what it meant. Hemingway taught a new generation of writers that less was more, that the reader could be trusted to bring experience to the story. No longer could one keep his distance from what was happening on the page. When Nick breaks "it" off with Marjorie beneath the rising moon, she forces him to say "it." Nick tells her "it" isn't fun any more, none of "it." Only after the reader has supplied his own antecedents for that ambiguous "it" does Marjorie ask, "Isn't love any fun?" To which question Nick replies only, "No." Even the title, "The End of Something," becomes more sardonic when the story is finished.

Almost single-handedly, Hemingway created a new, exciting mode for the American short story. Not everyone followed his lead, but so many writers learned from his work that today the Hemingwayesque story is commonplace. At its best, as in "The Killers," nothing happens. Violence is threatened but remains unfulfilled. Hemingway understood that the anticipation of violence is far more frightening than the violence itself. He also learned that conversation can carry meanings below its surface, that men and women speak in coded ways, that what is not said may be more important than what is said. Hemingway put understatement and irony to new uses in American fiction. At the close of *The Sun Also Rises,* the sexually charged Brett Ashley tells the sexually incapable Jake Barnes, "[W]e could have had such a damned good time together." Jake's laconic reply, the last words of the novel, are heavily freighted with ironic understatement: "'Yes,' I said. 'Isn't it pretty to think so?'"[7]

Although his general readers may not have noticed, Hemingway was continually conducting structural experiments, pushing the limits of the short story and the novel, exploring the possibilities of point of view. His depression-era novel, *To Have and Have Not,* is told in several voices, mixing first- and third-person points of view, counterpointing one narrative line with another. His now-classic short story "The Short Happy Life of Francis Macomber" breaks the genre's primary rule: never shift point of view. In that unhappy story, the point of view shifts from a detached narrator to the white hunter to Francis Macomber. The reader even knows what the lion is thinking as it makes its last charge. Hemingway handles these shifts so skillfully that they never disrupt the narrative flow. What the reader never knows, however, is what Margot Macomber thinks, for her point of view is never given. If it were, the never-to-be-resolved argument as to her intentions when she fires her rifle, killing her husband, would be over as soon as the reader finishes the story. Written in tandem with the Macomber story was Hemingway's other great African story, "The Snows of Kilimanjaro," in which he embedded several story fragments inside the narrative of the dying author, stories the character had never gotten around to writing, but which Hemingway, in telling the story, writes for him. "Snows" becomes a collection of short stories contained within a short story, which is structurally about as much freight as the genre will allow.

In his novel of the Spanish Civil War, *For Whom the Bell Tolls,* Hemingway did for the novel what he had done for the short story. He twists, bends, and sometimes breaks every tacit rule for the omniscient narrator. He moves into Robert Jordan's mind, an old prerogative, but then for extended periods, Jordan becomes the narrator, providing flashbacks to his earlier life and flash-forwards to fantasies of taking Maria to Madrid. Jordan's internal monologues turn into narratives, stories within stories, a decidedly postmodernist device, or an old Homeric device depending on one's orientation. Taking the process one step further, Hemingway lets many of the characters of the novel tell their own stories to the point that he recapitulates the effect of "The Snows of Kilimanjaro" by creating a collection of short stories embedded inside the novel.

Of the several hundred war novels written between 1914, when World War I began, and 1939, when Germany invaded Poland, only a handful have survived their first readers. In America, there are only two, both written by Hemingway: *A Farewell to Arms* and *For Whom the Bell Tolls.* Between them, he established the plot that drove almost every war novel and war movie between 1940 and 1960. The ingredients were basic. On the edge of the war zone, a soldier without a family falls in love with an attractive young woman. Changed by love, the soldier goes into battle, usually surviving in the movie versions to return to the woman who waits for him. Hemingway, who seldom wrote happy endings, brought sex and death together, changing the focus of the war novel. He created two male models: Frederic Henry, who becomes disillusioned with the war, and Robert Jordan, whose commitment sustains him to the point of death. Catherine Barkley is Frederic's strong, resourceful counterpart who hemorrhages to death in the Lausanne hospital. Robert Jordan dies protecting Maria's escape. In both war novels there is very little war, for Hemingway knew that large-scale battle was confusing and impossible to describe. Instead, he isolated small groups, letting their limited experience speak for the whole. Almost every American war novel written after 1940 has been influenced in some way by Hemingway's two paradigms, including his own variation on the earlier models, *Across the River and into the Trees.*

At another level, Hemingway's fiction marks the transition from modernism to postmodernism, for he is frequently writing about writing. In *For Whom the Bell Tolls,* Jordan, after listening to Pilar's story, thinks, "I wish I could write well enough to write that story." Time twists when the story within the story is listened to by a writer who hopes one day to write the story the reader has just read. Later, Jordan tells himself that he will write a book about the Spanish war, but to do it, he knows he will have to become a better craftsman. For Jordan to be a writer thinking about writing the story that is, in fact, being written by Hemingway cracks the realist's mirror, pushing the reader into terrain where fictions collapse into other fictions, their frames enclosed by other frames. Many of Hemingway's characters are writers: Nick Adams on the Big Two-Hearted River has left behind "the need to write"; Jake Barnes, a journalist, is self-consciously writing his novel; in "The Snows of Kilimanjaro," the writer, Harry, dying on the Serengeti Plain, bemoans the talent he has wasted; *To Have and Have Not* has its proletarian novelist, Richard Gordon; *Islands in the Stream* has a painter and novelist. In *The Garden of Eden,* David Bourne is torn between writing the story Catherine wants written and the stories about Africa he wants to write. Hemingway almost left his original ending on "Big Two-Hearted River," in which the character Nick says that he is the author of the *In Our Time* stories, including "Big Two-Hearted River."

Hemingway's influence on his contemporaries and those who followed was not limited to fiction writers. His nonfiction has affected journalists, sportswriters, outdoors writers, and natural historians. All of Hemingway's journalism written from 1920 to 1924 for *The Toronto Star*

The *Pilar* off Havana Harbor trolling for marlin. With his wounded right knee characteristically locked, Hemingway steers out into the Gulf Stream. He bought the *Pilar* in 1934, combining savings with an advance from *Esquire* magazine. Thirty-eight feet long and modified to his specifications, it is a fishing platform, not a pleasure boat. In 1942 the *Pilar* was refitted with a radio, detection gear, and armament to conduct antisubmarine patrols along Cuba's northeast coast.

has been collected in *Dateline: Toronto*. Most of his fishing and hunting pieces written for *Esquire* magazine between 1933 and 1936 have been republished in *By-Line: Ernest Hemingway*. His natural history of the bullfight, *Death in the Afternoon*, remains in print, as does his safari book, *Green Hills of Africa*. No American writer from Hemingway's era wrote so well about the physical sensations of fishing and hunting, about moving across terrain, about the flight of birds and the habits of marlin. To be with Nick on the river is to learn about trout fishing; to be with Ernest when the kudu breaks cover is for the reader to know what he will probably never have the chance to experience. In all forms of his writing, Hemingway travels to exciting places, relishes the food and drink, and describes the country, writing about travel as well as or better than anyone else. Although he never became the natural historian that he promised himself to become at age sixteen, he encompassed natural history in almost everything he wrote, including a naturalist's observations on the most dangerous game, his fellow man.

From the grave, Hemingway's posthumous publications continued to influence American writers to the end of the century. His memoir, *A Moveable Feast,* looks like a collection of short stories, mixing detail with the narrator's beautifully written but oftentimes vindictive sketches of the famous and the forgotten from his Paris years. Using all the techniques of fiction, this memoir blurs the distinctions between the genres. *The Dangerous Summer* had the same effect: part reporting, part meditation, part travel book, part biography. This breaking down of walls between genres has continued until the category "nonfiction" is almost empty, and the pretense of objectivity has all but disappeared. Hemingway's posthumous works may not have influenced books such as Norman Mailer's *Armies of the Night* (1968) or Truman Capote's *In Cold Blood* (1965), but he was certainly creating postmodernist fictions well before John Barth and company. Early in the twentieth century, physicists said that reality was subjective; as the millenium ended, that concept in subtle ways permeated the cultural landscape. Hemingway's posthumously published books written between 1946 and 1960 were one or two steps ahead of his time.

Nothing written lasts forever. Mark Twain's shelf of books has been reduced to *The Adventures of Huckleberry Finn* (1884). His contemporary, William Dean Howells, once Twain's equal, is now largely forgotten. Each decade that passes winnows more titles from contemporary memory. New classics replace older classics in current anthologies. It would, therefore, be foolish to predict which of Hemingway's works will be read a century from now, but more than a few have lasted to the end of the twentieth century. Of the fifty-four short stories published during his lifetime, almost a third have become and remain American classics. From *In Our Time,* his first collection, there are "Indian Camp," "The Doctor and the Doctor's Wife," "The End of Something," "The Battler," and "Big Two-Hearted River." From *Men Without Women,* "Hills Like White Elephants," "Fifty Grand," and "The Killers" are widely read. *Winner Take Nothing* has "A Clean, Well-Lighted Place," "The Light of the World," and "Fathers and Sons." Later came the two African stories, "The Short Happy Life of Francis Macomber" and "The Snows of Kilimanjaro." Perhaps no other writer has this many stories so firmly woven into the American cultural fabric. Of his several novels, *The Old Man and the Sea* remains his all-time best-seller, read worldwide in twenty different languages. *The Sun Also Rises* and *A Farewell to Arms* are not far behind.

Social scientists and historians quote from both novels when they write about the 1920s. Of Hemingway's lasting impact on this century, of this much one can be sure. In his stories and novels, Hemingway never shies away from man's inevitable fate: he loses, sooner or later, slowly or fast, and all he can do is choose his terrain, erect his ineffective defenses, and lose on his own terms. The lesson is timeless.

ADAPTATIONS OF HEMINGWAY'S WORK

THEATER: *A Farewell to Arms.* Laurence Stallings's adaptation opened at the National Theatre in New York on 22 September 1930 and closed after twenty-four performances.

The Fifth Column. Opened in New York the first week of March 1940 to mixed reviews. Hemingway's original text was revised by Benjamin F. Glazer to the point that Hemingway referred to the Broadway version as "*The Four Ninety-five Column Marked Down from Five.*"[8]

The Capital of the World. A. E. Hotchner's adaptation of this short story appeared on the television program *Omnibus* on 6 December 1953.

Cafe Universe (1999). Hotchner's adaptation of several Nick Adams stories.

There have also been several one-man Hemingway theater pieces, sometimes taken from his fiction, sometimes from his life.

BALLET: *The Capital of the World.* Music by George Antheil; choreography by Eugene Loring. The Ballet Theatre's presentation opened at the Metropolitan Opera House in New York on 27 December 1953. It first appeared on television on 6 December 1953 on *Omnibus.*

MOVIES: The best book on cinematic adaptations of Hemingway stories is Frank M. Laurence's *Hemingway and the Movies* (Jackson: University Press of Mississippi, 1981), from which comes most of the following information.

A Farewell to Arms (Paramount, 1932). Directed by Frank Borzage and starring Gary Cooper, Helen Hayes, and Adolphe Menjou. Hemingway refused to attend a premier of the movie and would not give Paramount public relations any help in publicizing it, for he had heard that in the picture Catherine Barkley did not die.

The Spanish Earth (CCM, 1937). Documentary filmed in Spain during the Spanish Civil War by director Joris Ivens. Hemingway was on location with Ivens and wrote the narrative for the voice-over. When Orson Welles's narration was judged inappropriate, Hemingway narrated the documentary.

For Whom the Bell Tolls (Paramount, 1943). Directed by Sam Wood and starring Gary Cooper, Ingrid Bergman, Akim Tamiroff, and Katina Paxinou. Hemingway made extensive revisions to the script, returning the dialogue to his original version and correcting egregious errors.

To Have and Have Not (Warner Brothers, 1944). Directed by Howard Hawks and starring Humphrey Bogart, Walter Brennan, and Lauren Bacall. William Faulkner worked on the script for the movie. The movie bears little resemblance to the novel.

The Killers (Universal, 1946). Directed by Robert Siodmak and starring Burt Lancaster, Ava Gardner, and Edmond O'Brien. This Mark Hellinger production is the only movie made from a Hemingway story which the author actually liked. He owned a copy of the movie at his home in Cuba.

The Macomber Affair (United Artists, 1947). Based on "The Short Happy Life of Francis Macomber," the movie was directed by Zoltan Korda and starred Gregory Peck, Joan Bennett, and Robert Preston.

Under My Skin (Twentieth Century-Fox, 1950). Directed by Jean Negulesco and starring John Garfield and Micheline Prelle, the movie was based on the short story "My Old Man."

The Breaking Point (Warner Brothers, 1950). A remake based on *To Have and Have Not,* the movie was directed by Michael Curtis and starred John Garfield and Patricia Neal.

The Snows of Kilimanjaro (Twentieth Century-Fox, 1952). Directed by Henry King and starring Gregory Peck, Ava Gardner, and Hildegarde Neff. Hemingway called this movie "The Snows of Zanuck," a sarcastic reference to producer Darryl F. Zanuck's revisions to the Hemingway story.

The Sun Also Rises (Twentieth Century-Fox, 1957). Directed by Henry King and starring Tyrone Power, Ava Gardner, Mel Ferrer, and Errol Flynn.

A Farewell to Arms (Twentieth Century-Fox, 1958). Directed by Charles Vidor and starring Rock Hudson, Jennifer Jones, and Vittorio De Sica. When producer David O. Selznick announced that he was changing the story to make the romance more believable, Hemingway was furious.

The Gun Runners (United Artists, 1958). Another remake based on *To Have and Have Not,* starring Audie Murphy, Eddie Albert, and Patricia Owens.

The Old Man and the Sea (Warner Brothers, 1958). Directed by John Sturges and starring Spencer Tracy. This was the only movie made from Hemingway's fiction in which Hemingway was actually involved. He worked closely with producer Leland Hayward and scriptwriter Peter Viertel to create what Hemingway hoped would be an accurate film. He insisted that real jumping marlin be used, not a rubber model in a back-lot tank. But he lost the battle: all of Tracy's scenes were shot on a Hollywood soundstage, and the close-up of the marlin was a rubber mock-up.

Hemingway's Adventures of a Young Man (Twentieth Century-Fox, 1962). Directed by Martin Ritt and based on several of the Nick Adams stories. Starring Richard Beymer, Diane Baker, Eli Wallach, and Arthur Kennedy.

The Killers (Universal, 1964). A remake based on the Hemingway short story, directed by Don Siegel and starring Lee Marvin, Angie Dickinson, John Cassavetes, and Ronald Reagan in his last movie role.

Islands in the Stream (Paramount, 1977). Directed by Franklin Schaffner and starring George C. Scott, David Hemmings, Gilbert Roland, and Claire Bloom.

NOTES

1. See chapter 2, "The Hero and the Code," in Philip Young, *Ernest Hemingway* (New York: Rinehart, 1952), pp. 28–50.

2. Michael Reynolds, *Hemingway: The Paris Years* (Oxford & New York: Blackwell, 1989), pp. 201–205.

3. See Bertram D. Sarason, *Hemingway and the Sun Set* (Washington, D.C.: NCR Microcard Editions, 1972).

4. See Reynolds, *Hemingway's First War* (Princeton: Princeton University Press, 1976).

5. Reynolds, *Hemingway: The 1930s* (New York: Norton, 1997), pp. 154–167.

6. *In Our Time* (New York: Macmillan, 1988), p. 34.

7. *The Sun Also Rises* (New York: Scribners, 1926), p. 259.

8. Carlos Baker, *Ernest Hemingway: A Life Story* (New York: Scribners, 1969), p. 338.

HEMINGWAY ON HEMINGWAY

Like many of his contemporaries (William Butler Yeats, James Joyce, Gertrude Stein, Ezra Pound, D. H. Lawrence), Ernest Hemingway was unusually aware that an author must also be his own best publicist. Or, as Wallace Stevens suggested, the artist not only must perform upon the stage, he first must build the stage that would contain and explain the artist's performance. Beginning with his earliest journalism, feature stories that included himself in some way, Hemingway began constructing that focusing stage until gradually in the public mind he replaced the man himself with the public performer.

The earliest of Hemingway's journalism written for the Oak Park and River Forest High School newspaper, *The Trapeze,* and his nascent fiction in the high school's *Tabula* magazine, has most recently been collected as *Hemingway at Oak Park High,* edited by Cynthia Maziarka and Donald Vogel Jr. (Oak Park, Ill.: Oak Park and River Forest High School, 1993). Earlier, Matthew J. Bruccoli edited a similar collection, *Ernest Hemingway's Apprenticeship: Oak Park, 1916–1917* (Washington, D.C.: NCR Microcard Editions, 1971). The Hemingway journalism written for the *Toronto Star* from 1920 to 1924 has been collected as *Dateline: Toronto,* edited by William White (New York: Scribners, 1985). The earlier *By-Line: Ernest Hemingway,* also edited by White (New York: Scribners, 1967), collected some of the *Star* stories along with the more important *Esquire* essays from 1933 to 1936, the North American News Alliance (NANA) reports on the Spanish Civil War (1937–1938), many of his World War II reports and essays (1941–1944), as well as his account of surviving two plane crashes in 1954. Thus, for any given part of his life, there exist his journalistic views on the period with himself at its center.

To read through Hemingway's journalism in chronological order is to read a personal history of the first half of the twentieth century as seen through the eyes of a trained, opinionated observer. As Philip Young once said, Hemingway's view of the world is frequently constricted but intense. It is like the view a man pinned down by machine-gun fire might

Bimini, 1937. Thirty-eight years old, with eight books published, Hemingway had become an admired and imitated author. Two months after this picture was taken, he appeared on the cover of *Time* magazine when his third novel, *To Have and Have Not,* was published. Heavier here than earlier, his beard and hair beginning to gray, squinting into the Bahaman sun, his face showed the effects of the strenuous life.

have through a crack in a stone wall: he may not see much, but he sees with clarity. Although Hemingway denigrated his journalism, saying it should not be reprinted, some of his reports on the conditions of his times are vintage Hemingway. His European stories for the *Toronto Star* are filled with precise images that epitomize larger issues. Hemingway saw the political issues that divided postwar Europe in concrete terms of people, places, and events. He wrote stories about the Italian Fascists, the devastating fall of the German economy, and the look of Christian refugees abandoning Thrace to the Muslim Turks.

> It is a silent procession. Nobody even grunts. It is all they can do to keep moving. Their brilliant peasant costumes are soaked and draggled. Chickens dangle by their feet from the carts. Calves nuzzle at the draught cattle wherever a jam halts the stream. An old man marches under a young pig, a scythe and a gun, with a chicken tied to his scythe. A husband spreads a blanket over a woman in labor in one of the carts to keep off the driving rain. She is the only person making a sound. Her little daughter looks at her in horror and begins to cry. And the procession keeps moving.[1]

Despite Hemingway's conviction that journalism's life span was measured in days, even hours, his two-year European coverage remains the best evidence of his developing point of view and his responses to the forces that shaped the century.

During the 1930s, when he was writing for *Esquire* magazine, Hemingway used the personal essay to discuss his travels in Europe and Africa, fishing in the Gulf Stream, the Italian invasion of Ethiopia, lessons in writing, and the coming of the next war. In the fall of 1935, he warned his readers,

> If there is a general European war we will be brought into it if propaganda . . . greed, and the desire to increase the impaired health of the state can swing us in. Every move that is made now to deprive the people of their decision on all matters through their elected representatives and to delegate those powers to the executive brings us that much nearer war.[2]

Never a lover of war, Hemingway urged that America avoid the European conflict that he saw as inevitable. It would not be our war, he said, and there would be no glory attached to it. "You will die like a dog," he wrote, "for no good reason."

Two years later he was in Spain reporting on the civil war being fought by the Loyalist government and Francisco Franco's invading rebel army. Backed by Nazi Germany and Fascist Italy, Franco had the artillery, the munitions, and the airplanes that eventually won the war, but not before journalists such as Hemingway exposed the horrors of air raids that bombed civilians and leveled villages:

[F]leet after fleet of bombers roared over Tortosa. When they dropped the sudden thunder of their loads, the little city on the Ebro disappeared in a yellow mounting cloud of dust. The dust never settled, as more bombers came, and, finally, it hung like a yellow fog all down the Ebro valley. The big Savoia-Marchetti bombers shone white and silvery in the sun, and, as one group hammered over, another came.[3]

To a world not yet engaged in total war, Hemingway's reports from Spain were graphic depictions of the World War to come. Dispassionate but not detached, Hemingway captured not only scenes from the battlefields, but also clear evidence of his own feelings.

In 1940–1941, almost a year before Pearl Harbor, Hemingway and his new wife, Martha Gellhorn, went to China to report on Chiang Kai-shek's defensive battle against the invading Japanese. After several weeks of muddy trails, uncomfortable boat rides, disease, rain, and assorted vermin, they returned to file their stories. Martha was most concerned with the effects of the war on the civilians. Ernest was more interested in the tactics, politics, and lessons of the war. He reported that the real war would come when the Japanese were defeated, for then the communist rebels of Mao Tse-tung and Chiang's nationalist army would square off. He also saw that Japan could not fight a large-scale war without an outside supply of iron ore, rubber, and gasoline, all of which were available in Malaysia, the Philippines, and Indonesia. Sooner or later, he said, Japan would move south to these resources. Then America would have to fight or lose access to the rubber so vital to its own rearmament. To reread Hemingway's dispatches from China is to realize how astute a military strategist he was.

In 1944 Hemingway went to World War II as a frontline correspondent for *Collier's* magazine. From England he took his readers on bombing raids over the German V-1 launch sites in France, and on V-1 intercept missions over the English Channel by night. On D day, June 6, 1944, he rode into the Fox Green Sector of Omaha Beach with a landing craft full of infantry, and lived to write a vivid description of the horrific confusion. *Collier's* readers traveled with him to the liberation of Paris and northward toward the last German defenses. At Hürtgenwald with the 22nd Infantry, Hemingway experienced and recorded the rain, the snow, the mined roads, and the deadly crossfire.

As a supplement to his journalism, Hemingway wrote several books of highly personal nonfiction, frequently bordering on the fictive. In *Death in the Afternoon* (1932), the major theme, the history and protocol of the bullfight, is counterpointed by the minor theme, the life and artistry of the writer. The implicit conclusion Hemingway asks the reader to make for himself is that the bullfighter and the writer are both artists with similar concerns, needs, and goals. Many of Hemingway's earliest and clearest accounts of his own writing can be found scattered through *Death in the Afternoon*. For example, it is here that Hemingway's now-famous iceberg metaphor was first explained in print.

Three years later, *Green Hills of Africa* suggested that the writer and the hunter are both in pursuit of beauty and truth. This highly structured book purports to be an attempt to see if "an absolutely true book" can "compete with a work of the imagination." In the narrative, Hemingway the author exposes the prowess and flaws of Hemingway the hunter. But he also allows Hemingway the writer to expound upon his trade, giving more information on his intent, his values, his reading, and his goals. Among the fallen animals, the lovely landscapes, and the camaraderie of camp life, the writer tells us what is necessary to achieve a prose not yet written.

At the very end of his life, Hemingway was at work on two very different factual/fictional presentations of himself. In the posthumously published *A Moveable Feast* he creates a portrait of the artist as a young man in Paris. This memoir sanctified many of the Hemingway legends—the young man poor in Paris; Hadley losing his manuscripts; going to Gertrude Stein's to see the modernist paintings on the wall; checking books out of Sylvia Beach's lending library; and writing in the cafés. "Some days it went so well that you could make the country so that you could walk into it through the timber to come out into the clearing and work up onto the high ground and see the hills beyond the arm of the lake."[4]

In the "fictional memoir" *True at First Light,* Hemingway returned to the writer/hunter set down in Africa, this time near the end of his life, where past memories and old desires mingle in the present tense of the African Eden. If the young writer in *A Moveable Feast* was an innocent in Paris, the older Hemingway in *True at First Light* lives in a fallen world. All men are exiles from the Garden of Eden, John Dos Passos once told him.

That part of his self-constructed life missing from his journalism, essays, and nonfiction books was developed in Hemingway's extensive correspondence, much of it written with an eye toward his future biographers and his place in literary history. Although at the very end of his life, while suffering from severe depression, he signed a statement forbidding publication of his letters, his mandate only called attention to the rich account of his life and times embedded in his correspondence. In 1981 *Ernest Hemingway, Selected Letters 1917–1961,* edited by Carlos Baker and

Interviewer: "What do you find wrong with present-day writing—or good about it? Why aren't we getting more significant writing?"

Hemingway: "Really good writing very scarce always. When comes in quantities everybody very very lucky."

Interviewer: "Has the 'Hemingway influence' declined? If so, what kind of writing are we heading for?"

Hemingway: "Hemingway influence only a certain clarification of the language which is now in the public domain."

From "Hemingway in the Afternoon," *Time*, 50 (4 August 1947): 80. Hemingway answered the interview questions by mail.

published by Scribners, provided the general reader with access to a judicious selection but by no means the entire body of Hemingway letters. Fifteen years later, the Hemingway sons allowed Matthew J. Bruccoli to edit the letters between Hemingway and his first Scribners editor, Maxwell Perkins. This collection of important letters detailing Hemingway's complex and often tumultuous professional life appeared as *The Only Thing That Counts* (1996). Eventually the complete letters of the author will be published, running to at least four volumes.

Finally, it is the Hemingway interviews that provide the mortar holding these bricks together in the Hemingway autobiography. Beginning with his return-from-the-war interview with the *New York Sun* in 1919 through his 1958 interview with George Plimpton, the most important of the Hemingway interviews have been collected by Bruccoli and published as *Conversations with Ernest Hemingway* (Jackson: University of Mississippi Press, 1986). Bruccoli has included the Hemingway's seldom-reprinted 1937 address to the American Writer's Congress, called "Fascism Is a Lie," and the author's Nobel Prize acceptance speech.

All told, reader and scholar have a rich if modulated self-exposure of how Hemingway became the public man and the famous writer: statements about his life, his art, his ups and downs, relationships with friends and wives, agony over books in progress, his vulnerability to critical barbs, his need for companions, the pleasures of drink, food, and country, where to go and how to get there, the look and feel of the Gulf Stream, the marlin strike, the fall of the kudu, the flow of the trout stream, and above all else his joy in life. It is a highly selective autobiography of a writer written over a lifetime, saying nothing of his depressions or most of his medical and marital problems. What he says about his art are statements of the ideal, the level he sometimes reaches but not always. The reader is cautioned to remember that Hemingway, like the reader, changes over time. Do not expect him to be at forty the young writer he was at twenty-five. Nor should anyone expect him to tell the bald truth, for he is a writer of fiction.

From his earliest publications, Hemingway was in continuous negotiation with his publisher over the inclusion of certain forbidden words, which he reluctantly allowed Scribners to replace with blanks, but he always argued for the full use of his native language. When Scribners published *The Sun Also Rises,* Hemingway was asked to make a number of changes. He replied:

> I never use a word without first considering if it is replaceable. . . . one place where Mike when drunk and wanting to insult the bull fighter keeps saying—tell him bulls have no balls. That can be changed—and I believe with no appreciable loss to—bulls have no horns. But in the matter of the use of the <u>Bitch</u> by Brett—I have never once used this word ornamentally nor except when it was absolutely necessary and I believe the few places where it is used must stand. . . . one should never use words which shock altogether out of their own value or connotation—such a word as for instance <u>fart</u> would stand out on a page . . . Altho I can think a case where it might be used, under sufficiently tragic circumstances, as to be entirely acceptable. In a certain incident in the war of conversation among marching troops under shell fire.[5]

> I've tried to reduce profanity but I reduced so much profanity when writing the book that I'm afraid not much could come out. Perhaps we will have to consider it simply as a profane book and hope that the next book will be less profane or perhaps more sacred.[6]

When Hemingway was asked by his editor, Maxwell Perkins, to write an introduction to *The Sun Also Rises* giving biographical background on some of the characters, he declined, saying,

> [A]ny sort of a forward or preface would seem to me to break up the unity of the book and altho it does not show there is a certain rhythm in all that book that if it were broken would be very much missed. . . . I think we'll find maybe, in the end, that what I lose by not compromising now we may all cash in on later. . . . I would like . . . to write books for Scribner's to publish, for many years and would like them to be good books—better all the time . . . as well as I could write and perhaps with luck learning to write better all the time—and learning how things work and what the whole thing is about—and not getting bitter . . . but I'll never be able to do that and will just get caught in the machine if I start worrying about . . . the selling.[7]

From his first meeting with F. Scott Fitzgerald's wife, Zelda, Hemingway thought she was detrimental to Fitzgerald's writing. Zelda had an equally low opinion of Ernest, calling him a phony. In a letter to Perkins, here is Hemingway on the topic of Zelda:

> I think 90% of the trouble he [Fitzgerald] has comes from her. Almost Every bloody fool thing I have ever seen or known him to do has been directly or indirectly Zelda inspired. . . . I often wonder if he would not have been the best writer we've ever had or likely to have if he hadnt been married to some one that would make him waste <u>Every thing</u>. I know no one that has ever had more talent or wasted it more.[8]

By 1929 Hemingway was once again in a battle with Scribners over the use of certain words in *A Farewell to Arms.* He was asked, for example, to take out the clinical details from Frederic Henry's hospitalization, including the word *bedpan*. He responded:

> About the words . . . Originally I had about 2,000 words of that aspect of hospital life—It really <u>dominates</u> it—I cut it all out with the exception of one reference to the bed pan.

It is the same with other words.

> You say they have not been in print before—one may not have—but the others are all in Shakespeare—

> But more recently you will find them in a book called All Quiet on the Western Front . . . with the word shit, fart etc. . . . I hate to kill the value of mine by emasculating it. . . . If a word can be used and is needed in the text it is a <u>weakening</u> to omit it.[9]

With *A Farewell to Arms* page-proofed but not yet published, Hemingway wrote Fitzgerald, complaining about his own letdown after finishing a book and trying to cheer up his friend:

> That terrible mood of depression of whether it's any good or not is what is known as The Artist's Reward. . . .

> Summer's a discouraging time to work—You dont feel death coming on the way it does in the fall when the boys really put pen to paper.

> Everybody loses all the bloom—we're not peaches—that doesnt mean you get rotten—a gun is better worn and with bloom off—So is a saddle—People too by God. You lose everything that is fresh and everything that is easy and it always seems as though you could *never* write—But you have more metier and you know more and when you get flashes of the old juice you get more results with them.[10]

When *A Farewell to Arms* was published with all its obscenities and vulgarities reduced to blanks, Hemingway was distraught, asking Perkins for one set of galleys with the words still in place.

> What I want to do is get them cut and bound up so I can have one copy of it as it was before the blanks. . . . I would rather write and then go over it and when I know it's right stick to it and publish it that way the way it was if it never sells a damned one—That's what I should have done. . . . I'm a Professional Writer

Hemingway with Martha Gellhorn, shortly before their marriage in November 1940. Nine years younger than Hemingway, Martha was a published young writer when she met Ernest in 1936. They had a four-year affair, conducted partly in Spain and Paris during the Spanish Civil War, where both were journalists, and married after Ernest's divorce from Pauline. Their marriage quickly deteriorated when Martha refused to become caretaker and manager of the Hemingway house.

now—Than which there isn't anything lower. I never thought I'd be it (and I'm damned if I'm going to do it any more)—But if I can get one copy of it and I can see I got it set up the way it was . . . in type it will take some of the curse off it.[11]

With the onset of the Great Depression, proletarian writers became popular with left-wing critics whose Marxist views were their newfound religion. Hemingway, who was never a follower, bristled at such programmatic writing. He told Paul Romaine

I do not follow the fashions in politics, letters, religion etc. If the boys swing to the left in literature you may make a small bet the next swing will be to the right and some of the same yellow bastards will swing both ways. There is not left and right in writing. There is only good and bad writing.[12]

To his old friend John Dos Passos, he wrote

I suppose I am an anarchist—but it takes a while to figure out. . . . I don't believe and can't believe in too much government—no matter what good is the end. To hell with the Church when it becomes a State and the hell with the State when it becomes a church. Also it is very possible that tearing down is more important than building up.[13]

To a Russian critic and admirer of his work, Hemingway explained in greater detail:

I cannot be a communist now because I believe in only one thing: liberty. First I would look after myself and do my work. Then I would care for my family. Then I would help my neighbor. But the state I care nothing for. All the state has ever meant to me is unjust taxation. I have never asked anything from it. . . . I believe in the absolute minimum of government. . . . A writer is like a Gypsy. He owes no allegiance to any government. If he is a good writer he will never like the government he lives under. His hand should be against it and its hand will always be against him. The minute anyone knows any bureaucracy well enough he will hate it. Because the minute it passes a certain size it must be unjust.[14]

During World War II, when writers were asked to publish statements supporting the war effort on the backs of their dust jackets, Hemingway balked:

I have decided . . . not to write any propaganda in this war at all. I am willing to go to it and will send my kids to it and will give what money I have to it but I want to write just what I believe all the way along through it and after it. It was the writers in the last war who wrote propaganda that finished themselves off that way. There is plenty of stuff that you believe absolutely that you can write which is useful enough without having to write propaganda.[15]

In one of his very few letters to a politician, Hemingway pulled no punches with Senator Joe McCarthy, who was then at the height of his powers:

I know you were in a fine force and you must have been wounded really badly but Senator you certainly bore the bejeesus out of some tax-payers and this is an invitation to get it all out of your system. You can come down here and fight for free, without any publicity, and with an old character like me who is fifty years old and weighs 209 and thinks your are a shit, Senator, and would knock you on your ass the best day you ever lived. It might be healthy for you and it would certainly be instructive.[16]

After several book reviews denigrated *Death in the Afternoon,* Hemingway was furious:

> I am tempted never to publish another damned thing. The swine arent worth writing for. I swear to Christ they're not. Every phase of the whole racket is so disgusting that it makes you feel like vomiting. Every word I wrote about the Spanish fighting bull was absolutely true and result of long and careful and exhaustive observation. Then they pay [Max] Eastman, who knows nothing about it, to say I write sentimental nonsense.[17]

Hemingway was in correspondence with several fellow writers— Archibald MacLeish, John Dos Passos, F. Scott Fitzgerald, and Lillian Ross. To Majorie Kinnan Rawlings, he explained his need for both the active and the contemplative life:

> As for being Sportsman being Artist. I always fished and shot since I could carry a canepole or a single barrelled shotgun; not to show off but for great inner pleasure and almost complete satisfaction. Have not been writing as long but get the same pleasure, and you do it alone, only it is a goddamned sight harder to do and if I did nothing else (no fish, no shoot, no drink) would probably go nuts doing it with the difficulty, the times in between when you can't do it, the always being short of what you want to do, the rest of it with all of which you have probably lived some time and various places.[18]

When sorting out a misunderstanding about public comments with William Faulkner, Hemingway wrote:

> You are a better writer than Fielding or any of those guys and you should just know it and keep on writing. You have things written that come back to me better than any of them. . . . You should always write your best against dead writers that we know . . . and beat them one by one. Why do you want to fight Dostoevsky in your first fight? Beat Turgenieff—which we both did soundly and for time which I hear tick too. . . . Then nail yourself DeMaupassant. . . . Then try and take Stendhal. . . . But don't fight with the poor pathological characters of our time. . . . You and I can both beat Flaubert who is our most respected, honored master. . . . Anyway I am your Bro. if you want one that writes and I'd like us to keep in touch.[19]

About his relationship with Gertrude Stein and her automatic writing, Hemingway said:

> [S]he only gave real loyalty to people who were inferior to her. She had to attack me because she learned to write dialogue from me just as I learned the wonderful rhythms in prose from her. I couldn't understand it when she attacked me but I did not give a damn really. . . . [S]he had discovered a way of writing she could do and be happy every day. She could not fail; nor strike out; nor be knocked out of the box because she made the rules and played under her own rules. When I can't write (writing under the strictest rules I know) I write letters. . . . She found a way of writing that was like writing letters all the time.[20]

In the 1950s, when would-be biographers began to hound Hemingway for his cooperation, he resisted as well as he was able, trying to keep them at a distance, for he feared that their intrusion into his life would jeopardize the source of his creative writing. Here, in two letters to Charles Fenton, are samples of his response:

> [Y]ou feel it is your duty as a scholar . . . to dig into my family while I am still alive. . . . Nobody in Oak Park likes me I should suppose. The people that were my good friends are dead and gone. I gave Oak Park a miss and never used it as a target. You wouldn't like to bomb your home town would you? . . . if I had written about Oak Park you have a point in studying it. But I did not write about it.[21]

> Mr. Fenton the trouble with a project like yours is that you in-evitably do not arrive at the true gen. You get survivours gen. . . . It is important that I should write about the Paris part as no-one knows the truth about it as I do and it is an interesting time in writing. . . . Any man's autobiography is his own prop-erty. He should have the choice of deciding whether he chooses to write it or not. But he should certainly not feed it piece-meal into letters for another man to use.[22]

In Hemingway's fiction and nonfiction, his numerous interviews and essays, and in posthumous summations of his life, one can find his trenchant comments on the condition of the writer in the twentieth century.

HEMINGWAY ON LEARNING TO WRITE

When a writer first starts out, he gets a big kick from the stuff he does, and the reader doesn't get any; then, after a while, the writer gets a little kick and the reader gets a little kick; and finally, if the writer's any good, he doesn't get any kick at all and the reader gets everything.(*The New Yorker,* 4 January 1947)

I found the greatest difficulty, aside from knowing truly what you really felt, rather than what you were supposed to feel, and had been taught to feel, was to put down what really happened in action; what the actual things were which produced the emotion. . . . the real thing, the sequence of motion and fact which made the emotion and which would be as valid in a year or in ten years or, with luck . . . always. . . . (*Death in the After-noon,* p.2)

So finally I would write one true sentence, and then go on from there. It was easy then because there was always one true sentence that I knew or had seen or had heard someone say. If I started to write elabo-rately, or like someone introducing or presenting something, I found that I could cut that scrollwork or ornament out and throw it away and start with the first true simple declarative sentence I had written. (*A Moveable Feast,* p. 12)

I went there [the Musée du Luxembourg] nearly every day for the Cézannes and to see the Manets and the Monets and the other Impressionists that I had first come to know about in the Art Institute at Chicago. I was learning something from the painting of Cézanne that made writing simple true sentences far from enough to make the stories have the dimensions that I was trying to put in them. I was learning very much from him but I was not articulate enough to explain it to anyone. Besides it was a secret. (*A Moveable Feast*, p. 13)

To keep my mind off writing sometimes after I had worked I would read writers who were writing then, such as Aldous Huxley, D. H. Lawrence. . . . [To Gertrude Stein:] "He wrote some very good short stories, one called 'The Prussian Officer.' . . . I liked *Sons and Lovers* and *The White Peacock.* . . . I couldn't read *Women in Love.* . . ." I read all the Mrs. Belloc Lowndes that there was. . . . [and] the good Simenons—the first one I read was either *L'Ecluse Numéro 1*, or *La Maison du Canal.* (*A Moveable Feast*, pp. 26–27)

HEMINGWAY'S ADVICE ON WRITING

[H]e [the aspiring writer] should go out and hang himself because he finds that writing well is impossibly difficult. Then he should be cut down without mercy and forced by his own self to write as well as he can for the rest of his life. At least he will have the story of the hanging to commence with. (*The Paris Review*, Spring 1958)

There is no use writing anything that has been written before unless you can beat it. . . . The only people for a serious writer to compete with are the dead that he knows are good. (*Esquire*, "Monologue to the Maestro," October 1935)

Sometimes you know the story. Sometimes you make it up as you go along and have no idea how it will come out. Everything changes as it moves. That is what makes the movement which makes the story. Sometimes the movement is so slow it does not seem to be moving. But there is always change and always movement. (*The Paris Review*, Spring 1958)

The best way is to read it all every day from the start, correcting as you go along, then go on from where you stopped the day before. (*Esquire*, "Monologue to the Maestro," October 1935)

The important thing is to work every day. I work from about seven until about noon. Then I go fishing or swimming, or whatever I want. The best way is to always stop when you are going good. If you do that you'll never be stuck. And don't think or worry about it until you start to write again the next day. That way your subconscious will be working on it all the time. (*Writer's Digest,* December 1964)

I always try to write on the principle of the iceberg. There is seven-eighths of it underwater for every part that shows. Anything you know you can eliminate and it only strengthens your iceberg. It is the part that doesn't show. (*The Paris Review,* Spring 1958)

When you walk into a room and you get a certain feeling or emotion, remember back until you see exactly what it was that gave you that emotion. Remember what the noises and smells were and what was said. Then write it down, making it clear so the reader will see it too and have the same feeling you had. And watch people, observe, try to put yourself in somebody else's head. (*Writer's Digest,* December 1964)

Good writing is true writing. If a man is making a story up it will be true in proportion to the amount of knowledge of life that he has and how conscientious he is; so that when he makes something up it is as it would truly be. (*Esquire,* "Monologue to the Maestro," October 1935)

[Y]our whole object is to convey everything, every sensation, sight, feeling, place and emotion to the reader. (*Esquire,* "Monologue to the Maestro" October 1935)

A writer, if he is any good, does not describe. He invents or *makes* out of knowledge personal and impersonal and sometimes he seems to have unexplained knowledge which could come from forgotten racial or family experience. Who teaches the homing pigeon to fly as he does; where does a fighting bull get his bravery, or a hunting dog his nose? (*The Paris Review,* Spring 1958)

From things that have happened and from things as they exist and from all things that you know and all those you cannot know, you make something through your invention that is not a representation but a whole new thing truer than anything true and alive, and you make it alive, and if you make it well enough, you give it immortality. (*The Paris Review,* Spring 1958)

Prose is architecture, not interior decoration, and the Baroque is over. For a writer to put his own intellectual musings . . . into the mouths of artificially constructed characters . . . does not make literature. (*Death in the Afternoon,* p. 191)

If a writer of prose knows enough about what he is writing about he may omit things that he knows and the reader, if the writer is writing truly enough, will have a feeling of those things as strongly as though the writer had stated them. . . . A writer who omits things

CERTIFICATE OF IDENTITY OF NONCOMBATANT
(Pars. 76, 94, and 100, FM 27-10)

APO 887, 20 May 1944
(Place and date)

The bearer, ERNEST M. HEMINGWAY, whose signature appears below, is hereby certified to be **Accredited War Correspondent.**

attached to the Army of the United States in the European Theater of Operations (~~Defense Command~~) and, as such, in event of capture by the enemy is entitled to be treated as a prisoner of war, and that ~~(s)~~he will be given the same treatment and afforded the same privileges as an officer (~~enlisted man~~) in the Army of the United States of the grade of

Captain

~~xxxxxxxxx~~ By order of Theater Commander

(Signature of holder)

SEAL   ELMER F. POELKE, 1st Lt. AGD _(Signature of issuing authority)_

IDENTIFYING INFORMATION

Age 45   Weight 220

Height 6 ft. — in.

Color of hair   Brown

Color of eyes   Brown

Hq.SOS.—23-11-43/21w/19102 (44/5 390027)

FINGERPRINTS—RIGHT HAND, IF OBTAINABLE

THUMB

1   2   3   4

New York, 20 May 1944. Not yet forty-five, despite what his identification card says, Hemingway reluctantly agreed to become a frontline war correspondent for *Collier's* magazine. Having spent two years working counterintelligence and leading coastal patrols in Cuba, he had given up being a participant to become an observer. In the next five months, he flew RAF missions, rode an infantry landing craft into Omaha Beach, and participated in the liberation of Paris.

because he does not know them only makes hollow places in his writing. (*Death in the Afternoon*, p. 192)

The great thing is to last and get your work done and see and hear and learn and understand; and write when there is something that you know; and not before; and not too damned much after. (*Death in the Afternoon*, p. 278)

HEMINGWAY ON THE PROFESSION OF WRITING

All a writer of fiction is really is a congenital liar who invents from his own knowledge or that of other men. I am a writer of fiction and so I am a liar too and invent from what I know and that I've heard. . . . I make the truth as I invent it truer than it would be. That is what makes a good writer or bad. If I write in the first person, stating it is fiction, critics now will still try to prove these things never happened to me. It is as silly as trying to prove Defoe was not Robinson Crusoe so therefore it is a bad book. (*True at First Light*, p. 94)

Memory, of course, is never true. (*Death in the Afternoon*, p. 100)

Madame, all stories, if continued far enough, end in death, and he is no true-story teller who would keep that from you. . . . If two people love each other there can be no happy end to it. (*Death in the Afternoon*, p. 122)

If a man writes clearly enough any one can see if he fakes. If he mystifies to avoid a straight statement . . . the writer takes a longer time to be known as a fake and other writers who are afflicted by the same necessity will praise him in their own defense. (*Death in the Afternoon*, p. 54)

Now a writer can make himself a nice career while he is alive by espousing a political cause, working for it, making a profession of believing in it, and if it wins he will be very well placed. . . . A man can be a Fascist or a Communist and if his outfit gets in he can get to be an ambassador or have a million copies of his books printed by the Government. . . . But none of this will help the writer as a writer unless he finds something new to add to human knowledge while he is writing. Otherwise he will stink like any other writer when they bury him. . . . The hardest thing in the world to do is to write straight honest prose on human beings. First you have to know the subject; then you have to know how to write. Both take a lifetime to learn and anybody is cheating who takes politics as a way out. It is too easy. (*Esquire*, "Old Newsman Writes," December 1934)

[T]he way to paint is as long as there is you and colors and canvas, and to write as long as you can live and there is pencil and paper or ink or any machine to do it with, or anything you care to write about, and you feel a fool, and you are a fool, to do it any other way. (*Green Hills of Africa*, p. 12)

[American] writers when they have made some money increase their standard of living and they are caught. They have to write to keep up their establishments, their wives, and so on, and they write slop. . . . [T]hey write when there is nothing to say or no water in the well. . . . Or else they read the critics. If they believe the critics when they say they are great then they must believe them when they say they are rotten and they lose confidence. (*Green Hills of Africa*, p. 23)

Writers should work alone. They should see each other only after their work is done, and not too often then. (*Green Hills of Africa*, p.21)

Survival, with honor, that outmoded and all-important word, is as difficult as ever and as all important to a writer. . . . A writer without a sense of justice and of injustice would be better off editing the Year Book of a school for exceptional children than writing novels. . . . The most essential gift for a good writer is a built-in, shock-proof, shit detector. This is the writer's radar and all great writers have had it. (*The Paris Review*, Spring, 1958)

To have the heart of a child is not a disgrace. It is an honor. A man must comport himself as a man. . . . But it is never a reproach that he has kept a child's heart, a child's honesty, and a child's freshness and nobility. (*True at First Light*, pp. 25–26)

Writers should stick together like wolves or gypsies and they are fools to attack each other to please the people who would exploit or destroy them. (*Time*, 4 August 1947)

HEMINGWAY ON READING

Hemingway was a voracious reader whose final library in Cuba contained roughly eight thousand volumes in numerous categories: fiction, biography, literary history, military history, Civil War history, espionage, poetry, geography, travel, dictionaries in several languages, Africa, big-game hunting, ocean navigation, Spain, bullfighting, guns, bird hunting, detective fiction, and cooking, to name a few. At several points in his career, he recommended specific reading to would-be writers.

If I knew that by grinding Mr. [T. S.] Eliot into a fine dry powder and sprinkling that powder over Mr. Conrad's grave Mr. Conrad would shortly appear, looking very annoyed at the forced return and commence writing I would leave for London tomorrow morning with a sausage grinder. (*transatlantic review*, October 1924)

Anna Karenina, Far Away and Long Ago, Buddenbrooks, Wuthering Heights, Madame Bovary, War and Peace, A Sportsman's Sketches, The Brothers Karamazov, Hail and Farewell, Huckleberry Finn, Winesburg, Ohio, La Reine Margot, La Maison Tellier, Le Rouge et le Noire, La Chartreuse de Parme, Dubliners, Yeats's *Autobiographies*. (*Esquire*, "Remembering Shooting-Flying," February 1935)

I cannot read detective stories any more unless they are written by Raymond Chandler. Mostly I read biography, accounts of voyages that seem true, and military writing . . . [I read] the *New York Times* and *Herald Tribune*. ("Important Authors . . . Speaking for Themselves," *New York Herald Book Review*, 8 October 1950)

Mark Twain, Flaubert, Stendhal, Bach, Turgenev, Tolstoi, Dostoevski, Chekhov, Andrew Marvell, John Donne, Maupassant, the good Kipling, Thoreau, Captain Marryat, Shakespeare, Mozart, Quevedo, Dante, Vergil, Tintoretto, Hieronymus Bosch, Brueghel, Patinir, Goya, Giotto, Cézanne, Van Gogh, Gauguin, San Juan de la Cruz, [and] Góngora. (*The Paris Review*, Spring 1958)

HEMINGWAY ON THE WRITER'S GOALS

It is a prose that has never been written. But it can be written, without tricks and without cheating. . . . First, there must be talent, much talent. Talent such as Kipling had. Then there must be discipline. The discipline of Flaubert. Then there must be the conception of what it can be and an absolute conscience as unchanging as the standard meter in Paris, to prevent faking. Then the writer must be intelligent and disinterested and above all he must survive. (*Green Hills of Africa*, p. 27)

"I've worked at it solid for seventeen months," said Hemingway of his new novel [*For Whom the Bell Tolls*]. "This one had to be all right or I had to get out of line, because my last job, *To Have and Have Not*, was not so good. . . . I start work each morning at 7:30 and work until about 2:30. The first thing I do when I'm writing a novel is read back through all that has gone before. That way I break the back of the job. Then I put the words in—like laying bricks. I write in longhand and don't try to make much time. I've tried this speed writing, getting it all down and then

FROM A HEMINGWAY OBITUARY

"If the word 'classical' still has any meaning except just as the opposite of 'romantic,' then we can say that Ernest Hemingway was a classical writer. He was terse, lucid, economical; he pared life down to what he took to be the essentials, and then worked with great care and concentration to embody these essentials in imaginative form. He had neither the romantic interest in the untypical nor the adventure-story writer's interest in action for its own sake."

John Wain

From *The Observer,* 9 July 1961, p. 21.

going over it, but the trouble is if you speed too much you don't know if you have a book or not when you've finished the first draft. . . . The thing wrong with *To Have and Have Not* is that it is made of short stories. I wrote one, then another when I was in Spain, then I came back and saw Harry Morgan again and that gave me the idea for a third. It came out as a new novel, but it was short stories, and there is a hell of a lot of difference. . . . I don't know how many more I'll do. But they say that when you're in your forties you ought to know enough and have enough stuff to do one good one. I think this is it." ("Ernest Hemingway Talks of Work and War," *New York Times,* 11 August 1940)

Sure, they can say anything about nothing happening in "Across the River," but all that happens is the defense of the lower Piave, the breakthrough in Normandy, the taking of Paris and the destruction of the 22d Inf. Reg. in Hurtgen forest plus a man who loves a girl and dies.

Only it is all done with three-cushion shots. In the last one I had the straight narrative; Sordo on the hill for keeps; Jordan killing the cavalryman; the village; a full-scale attack presented as they go; and the unfortunate incident at the bridge. . . .

In writing I have moved through arithmetic, through plane geometry and algebra, and now I am in calculus. If they don't understand that, to hell with them. ("Talk With Mr. Hemingway," *New York Times,* 17 September 1950)

The themes have always been love, lack of it, death and its occasional temporary avoidance which we describe as life, the immortality or lack of immortality of the soul, money, honor and politics. That is an oversimplification. But nobody has employed me to write 150,000 words between covers on any of these themes this morning. ("Talk With Mr. Hemingway," *New York Times,* 17 September 1950)

The country that a novelist writes about is the country he knows; and the country that he knows is in his heart. Culture is good to have. It is like a good 1/10,000 map. But you have to make your own attack, and remember that no classic resembles another. ("Talk With Mr. Hemingway," *New York Times,* 17 September 1950)

For we have been there in the books and out of the books—and where we go, if we are any good, there you can go as we have been. A country, finally, erodes and the dust blows away, the people all die and none of them were of any importance permanently, except those who practiced the arts. . . . A thousand years makes economics silly and a work of art endures forever. . . . (*Green Hills of Africa,* p. 109)

OBITUARIES AND TRIBUTES

Charles Poore, "Books: Hemingway," *New York Times* (3 July 1961)

"Prose is architecture, not interior decoration," Hemingway once said, "and the baroque is over."

In a way lucky for him, the baroque was not over. Against its weary, ornamented excesses the spareness of his style stood out. With that style he did something to change the course of storytelling in our century.

If it was a simple style it had the simplicity of a Bach fugue or a landscape by Cézanne. The thousand and one writers who—consciously or unconsciously—imitated its elementals found that out. Or were found out, 'way over in left field, by their peers and voluntary counselors.

None could quite catch his harmonies and cadences. Others wrote pages spattered with three-word sentence dialogues. Their pages fell apart. And when they also tried to share the wealth of his material they usually achieved something not so much like Hemingway as like the peculiar movie and television versions of his stories, which only achieved one unity. The unity of being flawlessly miscast.

He stands now, with William Butler Yeats and James Joyce, as one of the three most influential writers of an era.

An Enduring Meteor

He appeared in the sky of our literature like a meteor—and then stayed there. A strange way for a meteor to act. Yet as each book appeared, savants dutifully issued final announcements that he was burned out. The Nobel Prize judges apparently believed those announcements until they read "The Old Man and the Sea."

He was sustained as effectively by his enemies as by his friends. The millions who enjoyed his stories were not particularly troubled by his skill in writing about violence. They had probably noticed that the world around them was generally in a state of considerable turmoil and that he found patterns of significance in its embroilments. Also, he created some heroines who brought about vicarious fatalities of the heart.

France, summer of 1944. Hemingway and his jeep driver study a detailed terrain map. Hemingway is not wearing his required journalist's armband but does have on his captured German belt buckle bearing the motto "Gott mit uns" (God with us). Although he wrote several feature stories for *Collier's* magazine, he also assisted David Bruce of the O.S.S. in the defense of Rambouillet and was the confidant of field commander Charles "Buck" Lanham, whose 22nd Infantry took heavy losses at Hürtgenwald.

Those who candidly deplored Hemingway and all his works sacrificed awesome amounts of time to the documentation of their disapproval. They seemed to have read every word he wrote. Since no statute required them to do so, one wondered where they found marginal leisure to enjoy authors they wholeheartedly admired.

Nor should we disdain his parodists. After all, their splendid lampoons added paving stones to the road toward the Nobel Prize, even if those paving stones were delivered by air.

There is an unassailable mythology about any writer's themes and characters. In Hemingway's case the salient idea is that he wrote about big-gamesters, pugs, thugs, girls with long legs and tawny hair, soldiers of fortune and misfortune. And that's right, isn't it? Anyone who ventures to point out, say, that in civilian life the hero of "A Farewell to Arms" was an architectural student, or that the hero of "For Whom the Bell Tolls" was a schoolteacher, or that the hero of "The Sun Also Rises" was a working newspaper man with an editor barking at him through the other end of a cable, must be guilty of some sort of weakness for obnoxious irrelevance.

Hemingway was no dove for the lit'ry coteries, but he was a gregarious man. He had more friends than any other writer of his stature, in more astonishingly varied circles, from Africa to Montana, from Key West to New York to Madrid, Paris and the Venetian Plain.

Scornful of the Herders

He was aware that many wanted him to settle down and cultivate the suburbanalities. Once he wrote a parody of the clucking intellectual herdsmen of literary nationalism. It was spoken by a fishing-trip companion to Jake Barnes, the hero of "The Sun Also Rises."

"You're an expatriate," the man tells Jake. "You've lost touch with the soil. You get precious. Fake European standards have ruined you. You drink yourself to death. You become obsessed by sex. You spend all your time talking, not working. You're an expatriate, see? You hang around cafes."

Hemingway wrote that more than a dozen years too soon. In due course, events at Pearl Harbor and elsewhere would enable uprooted multitudes of Americans in uniform to find necessity's most bitter expatriation.

One of Hemingway's friends was Bernard Berenson, connoisseur of life in art, art in life, who called "The Old Man and the Sea" "an idyll of the sea as sea, as un-Byronic and un-Melvillian as Homer himself, and communicated in a prose as calm and compelling as Homer's verse. No real artist symbolizes or allegorizes—and Hemingway is a true artist—but every real work of art exhales symbols and allegories."

A hatful of pedants will find new allegories, new symbols, in Hemingway, year after year after year. They will be able to do that the more easily because the books will live on.

"Authors and Critics Appraise Works," *New York Times,* 3 July 1961

Archibald MacLeish, poet and playwright—"He was a master of English prose, the great stylist of his generation. He had an English idiom of his own, which imposed itself by its own validity on his contemporaries. Like all true idioms it was an idiom of the human spirit, not of the language alone. Writers in other tongues were influenced almost as much as those who wrote in English. Hemingway felt the pulse of the time and gave it an equivalent in words."

Lionel Trilling, critic and Professor of English at Columbia University—"His place in American literature is secure and pre-eminent. There is no one in the whole range of literature of the modern world who has a better claim than he to be acknowledged as a master, but it is in his short stories rather than in his novels that his genius most truly and surely showed itself."

Alfred Kazin, author and critic—"Probably no other American writer of our time has set such a stamp on modern literature. Hemingway was one of our true poets. He gave a whole new dimension to English prose by making it almost as exact as poetry, by making every word sound, by reaching for those places of the imagination where the word and the object are one."

James Thurber, author and playwright—"Hemingway was unquestionably one of the greatest writers of the century. It was once said

"Once writing has become your major vice and greatest pleasure only death can stop it. Financial security then is a great help as it keeps you from worrying. Worry destroys the ability to write. Ill health is bad in the ratio that it produces worry which attacks your subconscious and destroys your reserves."

Ernest Hemingway

From George Plimpton, "The Art of Fiction: Ernest Hemingway," *Paris Review,* 5 (Spring 1958): 60–89.

accurately of him that his contribution to literature was a certain clarification of the English language. Of himself, he once said, 'The thing to do is last and get your work done.' I met him only once and we went over to Tim Costello's and had a wonderful time and became brothers."

John Dos Passos, novelist—"He was one of the best of our time. I believe his original short stories will certainly last. He was a great stylist and a magnificent writer. I am sure that all of his work that I have read will stand up. He was indeed a magnificent writer and his contributions were large."

Van Wyck Brooks, author and literary historian, Chancellor of the American Academy of Arts and Letters—"His destiny has been to symbolize an age of unparalleled violence as no other American has symbolized it. He was in his way a typical American, and there was something permanently adolescent about him that stood for a certain immaturity in the American mind. He was a twentieth-century Mark Twain as he was also a twentieth-century Byron, but he was unquestionably a great writer, a great artist in prose, the inventor of a style that has influenced other writers more than any other in our time."

Lillian Hellman, playwright—"He was a wonderful writer. I read proof on his first book when I was a 20-year-old at Horace Liveright [the publishing house]. 'In Our Time,' his first collection of short stories, came in as a manuscript, and I remember the great joy of taking it home that first night. I still think it was his best book."

Oliver LaFarge, novelist—"The use of English without elaboration, the directness of statement, the clarity of his prose liberated me of an attempt to write in a 'literary' manner. I think his more recent writing fell off badly, but I think he will stand as one of the very great short-story writers, and one of the great novelists. His use of dialogue to tell a story was absolutely extraordinary."

Tennessee Williams, playwright—"To begin with a somewhat obvious statement, twentieth-century literature began with Proust's 'The Remembrance of Things Past' and with Hemingway's 'The Sun Also Rises,' since literary history has already established the fact that Joyce was not and never was meant to be an artist with a comparably wide audience. Hemingway never retired from his life into his workshop. He knew that an artist's work, the heart of it, is finally himself and his life, and he accomplished as few artists that have lived in our time, or any, the almost impossibly difficult achievement of becoming, as a man, in the sight of the world and time he lived in, the embodiment of what his work meant, on its highest and most honest level, and it would seem that he continued this achievement until his moment of death, which he would undoubtedly call his 'moment of truth,' in all truth."

J. B. Priestley, British novelist and playwright—"Hemingway had a tremendous influence on writers all over the world, and on the whole it was a good influence. He was a subtle writer with the ability to put his message over in a simple way. Mind you, I didn't always agree with his work."

Cyril Connolly, British author and critic—"I think Hemingway was one of the half-dozen greatest living writers, a Titan of the age we live in. I put him with Joyce, Eliot and Yeats among the real founders of what is called the modern movement in writing. I think he still had a great deal to say."

Carl Sandburg, poet and biographer—"He was a writer who profoundly influenced style in America in the novel and the short story. He got a style going among many fellows using short words. He had no stock heroes. He chose his own order of people to love. His was a peculiar wisdom, sometimes a little bit flagrant, but his own."

V. S. Pritchett, author and critic—"The thing that strikes me most in looking back over his writings was that he revived the vernacular tradition and this was a most important contribution to Anglo-American literature. He reintroduced speech as a way of conveying stories. The only writer we had at all like him was Kipling. His influence on the short story was enormous, wherever you go, whether in India, the Middle East or elsewhere, you find that the young writers have read his short stories and are trying to imitate him."

C. P. Snow, British novelist—"He was a great original artist whose influence has spread all over the world. No novelist in the world has produced such a direct effect on other people's writing."

Harvey Breit, critic and playwright—"He once told me he was working in a new mathematics, and I was skeptical. I thought that even great and simple men delude themselves. But it turned out he was working in it. He had staked out a unique terrain. Over and beyond the battle cries that meant so much to so many of us, over and beyond his categorical imperatives of 'nada' and 'courage' and the struggle to last, to hold out, to be just, to love a good friend, and put down a bad enemy, over and beyond all these consistent truths in his work, he had found a language. It was more than an ear that recorded; it was a marvelous medium, immutable, through which all his experience passed, and an essence of truth resulted. He was a poet, really a poet, through his prose."

John O'Hara—"I can't think of any other in history who directly influenced so many writers. Especially young writers."

Robert Frost, poet—"Ernest Hemingway was rough and unsparing with life. He was rough and unsparing with himself. It is like his brave free ways that he should die by accident with a weapon. Fortunately for us, if it is a time to speak of fortune, he gave himself time to make his greatness. His style dominated our story-telling long and short. I remember the fascination that made me want to read aloud 'The Killers' to everybody that came along. He was a friend I shall miss. The country is in mourning."

J. Donald Adams, "Speaking of Books," *New York Times,* 16 July 1961

He met a fitting, if unfortunate end; it would have been anti-climactic had Hemingway died in his bed. Death had grazed him often, in the kind of life he lived; indeed, so great was death's fascination for him, that he seemed at times to seek it.

He was, in any case, one of those people who are accident-prone. He suffered many, and certainly one would wish to believe that when death claimed him, it was by virtue of the last accident in a long series.

When a writer of such distinct and dramatic personality comes to the final curtain, one thinks first of the man himself—and then of what he wrote. That is the order in which I wish to speak of him.

It has been truly said that he was the Byron of our time—not only another handsome, gifted youth who found himself famous almost overnight but closely akin in temperament too, unlike as they were in many ways, both as men and writers. Both were fundamentally men of action who were at the same time endowed—or burdened, if you like—with a sensitivity which made them writers also. Scarred as Hemingway's powerful body was by one mischance or another, the skin was thin, physically and spiritually. There is a wistfulness about the eyes and mouth in some of the pictures taken in his last years, (notably in one by Karsh of Ottawa) that strikes to one's heart.

Dedicated artist though he was—a man fiercely devoted to his craft—and a more disciplined one than Byron, he was capable at times of the same contempt for writing as a way of life, and so he had to prove himself in other ways. It is a virus that attacks all writers who are constitutionally both doer and poet. Hemingway was both. Like Byron again, he craved sensation.

He would have applauded, if he read it, Byron's remark in his Journals: "The great object is sensation—to feel that we exist, even in pain. It is this 'craving void' which drives us to gaming—to battle—to travel—to intemperate, but keenly felt pursuits of any description, whose principal attraction is the agitation inseparable from their accomplishment."

Both Hemingway and Byron were passionate observers; both could identify themselves wholly with a cause, as Byron did over Greek independence, and Hemingway in his hatred of fascism. Finally, again like Byron, he will be remembered as much for the legend he wove about himself, as for the best of what he wrote.

Though we never met, I had some correspondence with him in recent years which was sufficiently revealing, I think, to warrant mention here. Partly, this came out of a mutual love for the Rocky Mountain country, and aside from the manner of his death, I think it fitting that he died and will be buried in Idaho, his final choice of a home. We had something of an argument as to whether the Big Horns have foothills, but let that pass.

Hemingway's last wife, Mary Welsh, pictured while hunting in Idaho. Nine years her husband's junior, Mary was twice married and on her way to her second divorce when she met Ernest in wartime London, where she was a by-lined journalist for *Time* and *Life*. They began an affair that moved from London to Paris when it was liberated in August 1944. After Hemingway's divorce from Martha Gellhorn, he and Mary were married in Havana in 1946.

Writing to him eight years ago, I expressed the hope that he would some day do a novel about the Far West. In answer he said that his wife had been urging him to do so ever since he took her out to Wyoming, adding, "But I thought 'The Big Sky' was so good I wouldn't have to do it."

When I wrote to tell him how much I liked "The Old Man and the Sea," he replied: "I love the hills and the sea about the same. When

I'm either place I can't stand to leave. . . . I don't know how it is with you, but every time I come back from being at sea everybody seems kind of phony. It is the same way up in the hills.". . .

He was the greatest descriptive writer of our time, and in this his economy of words, and his choice of them, was as superb as Kipling's, and sometimes better. He gave a new dignity and strength to the American short story. Beside his best work in that field, the contemporary fuss over Scott Fitzgerald seems faintly ridiculous. Fitzgerald, for all his gifts, never approached, in that form, the mastery that Hemingway achieved. Hemingway was a master of mood, of atmosphere, and these are, perhaps, the basic qualities of the great short story.

It is, indeed, his possession of that gift that gives distinction to the best of his novels. That is the aura that clings to "The Sun Also Rises," however inconsequential most of its people are; it is what makes the poignancy of "A Farewell to Arms," what broods over "For Whom the Bell Tolls," and lends an overpowering unity to "The Old Man and the Sea." It is present now and then even in his inferior works, like "Across the River and Into the Trees." And that is why I referred to him earlier as a poet. There have been great novelists who were untouched by poetry—Balzac was one, Dreiser another.

There are debits in the accounting, of course, but I shall not dwell on them here. He was not a thinker. He did not, on the evidence of his novels, understand women or their relations with men; he did not understand the social, political and economic currents of his time. He never achieved emotional maturity or a balanced view of human life. But he was a great writer nonetheless, and an artist to the bone. He will have a lasting place, not only in American literature, but in that of the world. As a writer of determined convictions, he might delete half the adjectives in this piece about him, but I shall let them stand.

Carlos Baker, "A Search for the Man As He Really Was," *New York Times,* 26 July 1964

Ernest Hemingway used to remark that he did not want his biography written while he was alive, and preferably for 100 years after his death. During his lifetime, he did what he could to discourage his admirers from such an enterprise and to scare off his detractors with threats of legal action or more direct forms of dissuasion. In 1958, as a further non-incentive, he prepared a special document which served notice on his heirs that none of his letters was ever to be published. His widow and literary executrix, Mary Hemingway, has been holding as closely as possible to this directive, though sometimes, as in a recent issue of the *Mercure de France,* some letters have got into print simply because Hemingway's wishes are not universally known or respected.

Since he was one of the giants of his time, his wishes in the matter of biography have not been universally respected either. Seven or eight are already in print, and others may be expected. Whatever we may think of the quality and accuracy of these publications (and they do vary considerably in these respects), they were all plainly inevitable. For, by the act of dying, Hemingway surrendered control over his life in a double sense. Now he belongs, if not to the ages, at least very much to the age which in special ways he helped to fashion. Many of us would sooner keep on reading new works by Hemingway for as long as they last, or returning to old ones to see how they stand up under the weathering of the years. It is still a useful project to try to discover, in some systematic fashion, what he did for his epoch and what his epoch did for him.

Like most other human beings, Hemingway was both representative and unique. In working with the materials of his biography, one is chiefly struck by the uniqueness. Even though he would scorn the comparison, or find some way of turning it into a sardonic joke, what Ariosto said in "Orlando Furioso" applies here very well: "Nature made him, and then broke the mold." The mold that fashioned Hemingway lies broken today in a hundred thousand pieces.

The challenging task for any biographer who wishes to do his job well is to reassemble these fragments in such a way that this man, known in his day to millions though very well known only to dozens, can be made to return among us as a living being. In any absolute sense the task is of course impossible. The revivification of Lazarus was miraculous by definition. All that can be legitimately expected from even the most wonder-working biographer is an approximation of what Hemingway actually was.

One huge obstacle to seeing him plain is the pile of inexact allegations which bulk on the biographical horizon. For years he refused to give out any information about his personal life. Many commentators, lacking the data they thought they needed, felt obliged to invent whole episodes, people, relationships, adventures. Rumors rose like poltergeists, went the rounds, grew tired, lay down and calcified to monumental stone. Others, seeing them recumbent, took them for fact, and now they have become part of literary history. The biographer must, however, take the greatest pains to reject them. With every available device from

"Ernest Hemingway was a highly readable writer, one whose stories lost no time in communicating themselves from the printed page to the reader, from dialogue on paper to dialogue sounding in one's own ears and carrying his tales forward as if the characters were alive and *right there* in person. The immediacy of Hemingway's reality conveys itself with more than deliberate speed, and with an impact few other writers so quickly and so compactly achieve. Some commentators said years ago that Hemingway was a writer's writer. He turned out to he a reader's writer as well."

Langston Hughes

From *The Mark Twain Journal*, II (Summer 1962)

tweezers to bulldozers he must clear away the detritus of falsehood. Only then is there a chance of seeing the man as he actually was.

The attempt to recapture the colors and shades of his unique ambiance sends the biographer first of all to those who knew him best. One of the rewards of working with the life of a contemporaneous writer is the people one meets in the course of investigation. Though Hemingway made a substantial group of enemies, both by accident and intent, he was generally lucky in his friendships, luckier still in the lasting loyalties he was able to command. The number of those who kept in touch with him for a period of up to 40 years is far greater than is common among us. He grew away from many, of course, as many did from him, evidence of which is amply provided in the pages of his posthumous volume, "A Moveable Feast." To others he displayed an astonishing continuity of affection. Even those who felt, on occasion, the full weight of his anger usually prove on closer acquaintance to be magnanimous men and women, remembering with minimal rancor the years and adventures they shared in his company.

To name them here would be invidious. But it is from people like these—jai-alai players, maharajahs, soldiers, ex-wives, hunting-guides, metropolitan columnists, veterans of the Abraham Lincoln Brigade, movie stars, ski-meisters, toreros, circus bear-trainers, restaurateurs and a scattering of literary people—that one gradually assembles the motes of light and heat which made up the atmosphere in which Hemingway lived and moved. From them it is possible to learn ever more deeply about that curious blend of seriousness and lightheartedness, paternalism and boyishness, firmness and gentleness which counteracts in most of their memories, the wild-boar truculence, the gratuitous cornadas, the surly threats and contemptuous insults of which he was likewise capable.

The biographer, wearing his special monomania like a judge's cloak, regularly asks Hemingway's former associates to perform feats of memory worthy of a courtroom witness under oath. He often requires more of them than he could himself achieve. But he soon develops a rough system of overlapping chronologies, incontrovertible (and therefore trustworthy) places and dates, and other schema which can serve as crutches for limping rememberers. As soon as they are convinced of the biographer's need for truth, most witnesses will labor mightily to help him attain precision.

Yet even with the best witnesses, the biographer must harbor, along with his will to believe, a healthy determination to remain skeptical until a case is proved. He may not go as far as Hemingway himself, who remarked long ago that "memory . . . is never true." But he will not go very far in his work before he discovers that interviewing, per se, is never enough. This is why the basic groundwork for any trustworthy biography ought to be a wide and well-organized collection of letters to and from the subject.

Nothing, in fact, helps a biographer more than letters. Note even formal autobiography is quite so revealing as the relaxed, informal words a man sets down at a particular place and time for the eyes of a friend. If it were possible to gather under one roof the absolute total of any person's correspondence from kindergarten to coffin, his biographer's task would be considerably eased. Most of those who try to trace another's tracks through space and time must, however, settle for a record far less than perfect. For we are not always writing letters, nor do all our letters survive, nor do we reveal in what we write more than a fractional part of what we are even then thinking and feeling.

There are bound to be gaps and lapses, indecipherable runes and wordless tunes—those mysteries, as someone said, which lie (and lie and lie) near the heart of all our histories. Even though the biographers' skepticism must therefore operate on the testimony offered by letters, he cannot afford to abandon for a moment his perpetual search for communications by, to, or about the subject of his interest.

Hemingway was, luckily, an indefatigable letter-writer. Nearly to the end of his life he took pleasure in the exchange of news, gossip, plans, dreams and nightmares. His letters are full of boasts, self-recriminations, confessionals, complaints and high and low badinage. After a day's work—say 753 words set down in four hours—he often turned to letters as a means of braking down his slow-moving equipage while the wheels of his imagination still lumbered forward. It was, he found, a better means of unburdening himself than a psychiatrist's couch. It skimmed his boiling brain of non-essentials, settled (or sometimes complicated) his business affairs, helped to alleviate his black rages, answered his need for comradely interchange with friends he trusted, explained himself to himself, and helped to exhaust him so that he could sleep.

Havana, March 1956. Left to right: Two Cuban friends, Hemingway's son Jack, actor Spencer Tracy, Ernest, and Mary occupy Hemingway's favorite corner of the Floridita Bar. Tracy, who this night fell off the wagon, was in Havana to complete the filming of *The Old Man and the Sea.* Anxious that the picture be true to life, Ernest and Mary provided support for the film crew. In front of Ernest is his favorite "Papa doble" daiquiri.

The loss or preservation of these crucial documents is often, and unfortunately, a matter of luck. Juanito Quintana, proprietor of the Pamplona hotel which Hemingway immortalized as the Montoya in "The Sun Also Rises," lost both his establishment and all but five of his letters from Ernesto during the Spanish Civil War. Margaret Anderson, editor of *The Little Review,* lost hers when the Germans occupied Paris. Other batches have been burned, inadvertently dumped, eaten to shreds by tropical insects, made illegible by damp-rot while the owner was away fighting in the Aleutians, or they have simply vanished into the insatiable maws of trunks in forgotten attics. On the other hand, it is posterity's good fortune that Mary Welsh Hemingway chose to take her obligations as executrix so seriously that all her husband's papers from Cuba, Florida and Idaho have now been sorted, classified, placed in folders and preserved for future reference.

Sometimes the most tentative of queries can uncover a treasure trove. There is, for example, the case of a former secretary of Hemingway, who not only saved all her stenographic notebooks but also discovered, to her considerable astonishment, that she could still read her shorthand notes after the lapse of years. That she was willing to make a tape recording of these letters for the benefit of Hemingway's biography still seems to his biographer one of the happier eventualities of the century.

Less significant, though amusing enough, is the existence in a generous collector's hands of a set of three letters, two of them by Hemingway and the third by a young British novelist-journalist who once asked to interview the master in his Cuban home. Hemingway politely declined, suggesting that the young man could get what he needed from a close friend in New York, and enclosing a letter of introduction to that friend. The young Englishman, short of cash and completely unsentimental, promptly sold his little sheaf for what they would bring in the open market, pocketed the cash, and moved on to interview someone else.

So the biographer will do well to count on letters, at least up to a point. They are certainly indispensable to the establishment of biographical exactitude. Yet even the information they contain must be examined with skepticism and used with caution. For it is a curious human tendency to tell lies in letters, fitting the text to what one knows of the recipient, withholding what one doesn't want known, skating with aplomb over the acres of thin ice. People of the most exemplary rectitude fall easily into this habit, and often for the best of reasons.

It should therefore not surprise us to find in the letters of a practicing novelist, for whom the line between fact and fancy is a many-splendored nonentity, some visible discrepancies between the truth as it was and the truth as he saw it. We all live by private mythologies. One of Hemingway's, of which he apprised his friends for years, was that his second novel was published the day the stock market crashed. Frequent repetition seems to have convinced him that this was so, though the volume had been on sale for more than a month before the dawn of the Great Dark Day.

A third source of biographical data which must be treated with more than usual circumspection is Hemingway's fiction itself. One important plank in his esthetic platform was the writer's obligation to tell the truth. This meant, in fictional practice, that he seldom wanted to depart very far from events in which he had played some personal part. The blowing up of Frederick Henry in "A Farewell to Arms" is based, for example, directly on Hemingway's own encounter with an Austrian Minnenwerfer on the Piave front one July midnight in 1918. Beyond the central incident, however, the biographer must watch for booby-traps. The actual and the imagined are everywhere so tightly interwoven that disentanglement is virtually impossible.

Other entanglements are somewhat easier to straighten out. One instance occurs near the end of "For Whom the Bell Tolls," where Robert Jordan is made to recall a family wedding in which he participated as a child—a memory closely associated with the spectacle of a Negro hanged on a lamp-post. Was this something Hemingway remembered from his childhood? No, as it turns out. He had picked up the story from his sister Marcelline, who served as a flowergirl at the wedding of her aunt and uncle in an Ohio town close to the turn of the century. One of her graphic memories of the otherwise festive occasion was a glimpse of a murdered man. Almost 40 years later her brother appropriated the incident as part of Jordan's background.

Widely variant combinations of truth and fiction appear in the stories. The setting for the prize-winning "My Old Man" is completely authentic, based on Hemingway's own race-track experiences in Milan and Paris. All the rest is invented. So is the famous story called "Indian Camp," where Dr. Adams performs a Caesarean section on an Indian squaw, using a jackknife as a scalpel and a gut-leader as a suture. On the other hand, "The Doctor and the Doctor's Wife" is virtually a playback of an actual quarrel between Dr. Hemingway and a halfbreed Indian sawyer on the shore of Walloon Lake in the summer of 1912, with the youthful Ernest Hemingway as an interested onlooker. This is proved by a letter from his father to Ernest, written some 13 years after the event.

Frederick Bush, "Reading Hemingway Without Guilt," *New York Times*, 12 January 1992

It is not fashionable these days to praise the work of Ernest Hemingway. His women too often seem to be projections of male needfulness. There are too many examples of his lifelong anti-Semitism, his affection for denigrating black people in just too many forums private and public. And he was violent: he loved the bullfights, he wrote of them with zeal, explaining away the cruelty to bulls and horses by celebrating how the matador danced with death.

And he was just plain mean. As we reread "A Moveable Feast," we experience Hemingway's ingratitude, his viciousness to Ford Madox

Ford, to F. Scott Fitzgerald, to Gertrude Stein; and when we consider his treatment of Stein, we have to recall Hemingway's defamation of homosexuals.

He is so very incorrect, except in this: he gave the century a way of making literary art that dealt with the remarkable violence of our time. He listened and watched and invented the language—using the power, the terror, of silences—with which we could name ourselves.

Often, he employed an apparently cocky but clearly shattered persona, as in this passage from "In Our Time": "When they evacuated they had all their baggage animals they couldn't take off with them so they just broke their forelegs and dumped them into the shallow water. All those mules with their forelegs broken pushed over into the shallow water. It was all a pleasant business. My word yes a most pleasant business."

This persona contained the tension, as a nervous laugh contains a terrible cry, that was the heart of Hemingway's method. The voice he invented could suggest the sorrow of the violence perceived while attempting to create repose, an instant's peace. The voice carried the violence and the flight from it simultaneously.

We can hear the simultaneity in the splendid opening paragraph of "A Farewell to Arms" (1929), a first paragraph that is a reworking of the opening lines of the 1926 story "In Another Country":

> In the later summer of that year we lived in a house in a village that looked across the river and the plain to the mountains. In the bed of the river there were pebbles and boulders, dry and white in the sun, and the water was clear and swiftly moving and blue in the channels. Troops went by the house and down the road and the dust they raised powdered the leaves of the trees. The trunks of the trees too were dusty and the leaves fell early that year and we saw the troops marching along the road and the dust rising and leaves, stirred by the breeze, falling and the soldiers marching and afterward the road bare and white except for the leaves.

The paragraph is resonant, haunting, a poem: it contains the movement of the novel, it predicts the lovers' fate, and it then transcends their fate, on our behalf, by creating a moment that survives them.

When he writes very well about love, loss, tenderness or fear, Hemingway works with the assumption that he must cause the reader to share the unstated emotion. That is responsible writing, a writing that is about the essential transaction between writer and reader. It is about being human in a time of despair.

Hemingway made it clear to his readers that a writer who stared into the truths or evasions of the soul and tried to bring back something of what he had seen was a comrade in arms to the warrior or hunter: each was a laborer at his trade who risked his life in the plying of the trade. Hemingway's work demonstrates that the making of art is a matter of life and death, no less.

At about the age of 24, I would say, Hemingway started to write about the choice his protagonists must make: either fall prey to the terror of living, and therefore kill themselves, or soldier on with what they might call professionalism. The choice was that severe. It was no metaphor. When he offered death as an alternative, Hemingway meant death.

He was a child of a doctor and a hardy, demanding artist (she had been a singer) who thought it important that their children see the dark facts of a difficult world. His father killed himself. Hemingway's first wife, Hadley, was the child of a suicidal father. When Hemingway was severely wounded during his Red Cross service at the Italian front in 1918 and he lay bleeding from many wounds, awaiting an ambulance and in terrible pain, he thought, at 19, of shooting himself with his sidearm. When he was leaving Hadley for Pauline Pfeiffer in 1926, he wrote to Pfeiffer of how he had thought "to remove the sin out of your life and avoid Hadley the necessity of divorce . . . by killing myself."

A month before, he had written to someone else that "the real reason for not committing suicide is because you always know how swell life gets again after the hell is over." The dark call to die, and the insistence upon continuing, like the offering and withdrawing of emotion in his fiction, is the essential rhythm of Hemingway's life and art. He was a nexus for death. After he had killed himself, his sister Ursula committed suicide in 1966 and his brother, Leicester, in 1982. In 1983, Adriana Ivancich, whom Hemingway had loved and on whom he modeled Renata in "Across the River and Into the Trees," also killed herself.

In his work, the expression of the dialectic begins in the story "Indian Camp" in his "In Our Time" (1925). It is a small, simple story: Dr. Adams, on vacation with his brother and his son, a very young Nick, is summoned to an Indian settlement in northern Michigan. A woman has been in agonizing labor for three days, and she suffers so loudly that "the men had moved off up the road to sit in the dark and smoke out of range of the noise she made." She lies on the lower bunk, while her husband, his foot so badly cut with an ax three days before that he cannot be moved, is pinned in place in the bunk above her.

Nick learns—he starts to learn—about birth and death. His father tries to explain about labor and how the woman's contractions are related to her screams. "I see," Nick says, lying. And then the woman cries her agony again, and Nick begs, "Oh, Daddy, can't you give her something to make her stop screaming?"

This is a story in a book of stories in which women—and, surely, pregnant women—are invasive. It is a book that is in part about eluding women. But it is also the book of Nick Adams's education to more than men without women. So it is essential when Dr. Adams replies, first, that he hasn't any anesthetic, and then: "But her screams are not important. I don't hear them because they are not important."

After the doctor performs a Caesarian with a jackknife and fishing leaders, and the infant is delivered, he examines the husband.

"The Indian lay with his face toward the wall. His throat had been cut from ear to ear. The blood had flowed down into a pool where his body sagged the bunk. His head rested on his left arm. The open razor lay, edge up, in the blankets."

While Dr. Adams does not hear the screams "Because they are not important," the husband must hear the screams. He cannot move away—he is pinioned by his maimed foot; he is caught in his life. Of course, Dr. Adams does hear the screams; he is physically closer to the woman than her husband is. He is telling Nick that he chooses not to hear them. When he exults over the success of his surgery, he also celebrates his ability to focus on his own psychic survival.

Ruined legs, the therefore inescapable screams, are repeated in Hemingway's work. They provide the basis for his characters' choices—for Hemingway's measurement of the success of their action and for their own measurement, too. Immobilized in pain and dread, they must respond to the screams that life forces upon (or from) them by killing themselves; or they must find a way of diminishing the impact of the screams while still performing in their threatened lives with generosity, courage and skill. They cannot flee "to sit in the dark and smoke out of range of the noise"—except by taking their own lives.

Hemingway was a writer who made the ethos of his fictive world a matter of living or dying. He chose not to confine the trials and esthetics of his characters (or of himself as writer) to matters of comfort or ambition. He insisted that writing—which to him and his characters was risky and even heroic—was itself a matter of living or dying.

The equation—living or dying with writing well or badly—continued, in "Death in the Afternoon" (1932) and "Green Hills of Africa" (1935). Hemingway mingles discussion of how to write honestly with how to face death.

No small part of Hemingway's artistic success and emotional appeal lies in his ability to announce pain and renounce it virtually in the same breath. He generates feeling and then his characters shy away from it; he and his characters are alive to pathos but labor to resist its attractions.

It can be argued that Hemingway's is the tactic of the child who seeks attention but who also wishes to avoid responsibility for having claimed it. It may be argued as well that the lover who labors to attract the beloved, and the artist who works for the affection or at least interest of the reader, may employ the same behavior.

The work remains, the art functions, and once we have praised ourselves for calling Hemingway a baby, we probably must come around to saying that the baby's fiction works awfully effectively on the soul of a reader who is not rigidly, ideologically insensible to it. We feel the emotion in the stories, and we feel the retreat from it.

In 1936, Hemingway was married to the very wealthy Pauline and consorting with members of her equally affluent circle; he had come to regard himself with distrust. He felt that he was not writing enough or well enough and that he had surrounded himself at his peril with the idle rich. He claimed to be unaffected by accusations that he was insensitive to the needs of the masses, though he did growl at his accusers. He wrote a draft of a story about a writer named Henry Walden who is dying in Africa of gangrene contracted from a scratch on the leg. The story was called "A Budding Friendship," and demonstrates ironically how the closer the writer came to death, the closer he came to the authentic self he had abandoned; for, as death approaches, the sick man, unable to hold a pencil, "writes" in his mind: despite the screams, he tries, finally, to do his job.

Hemingway, in later revision, abandoned Thoreau, called his writer Harry, retitled the story "The Snows of Kilimanjaro," and revisited his childhood, youth and young manhood. He concluded with a hallucinated voyage—it is ostensibly toward rescue but is really into death—that evokes Hemingway's own flight from the African plains to Nairobi when he was ill with dysentery.

At the story's start, when his wife asks how she can help him, Harry says, "You can shoot me. You're a good shot now. I taught you to shoot, didn't I?" Calling his gangrene "rot," and thereby evoking his moral deterioration as well, Harry says that rather than eat, "I want to write." That is his nourishment, and now that he is on the verge of death it is the only reason he wants to live: to write what he has failed to write.

As he dies, he senses death: "It had moved up on him now, but it had no shape any more. It simply occupied space." It has been, in his hallucinations, "two bicycle policemen . . . or a bird"; "it can have a wide snout like a hyena." He is beyond images by now, however. Death becomes, simply, "it," and is only a weight on his chest, beyond his powers to name or describe. As he fails as a writer, he dies.

Hemingway had heard a story about a frozen carcass of a leopard on Kilimanjaro and had used it as an epigraph to his story. It is his symbol, not his reader's: we can assign a variety of meanings to it, but they do not add to the richness of the story; at best, they can please us by seeming to confirm what we feel Harry's failure and dreams to mean. Hemingway believed that the weight of a story is created by the bulk of it being known only to the writer. Hemingway's epigraph may well have been intended as Hemingway's epitaph. The image of the leopard dead on Kilimanjaro is part of his trying to evade the screams, perhaps, or part of his giving in to them. Surely, the image is part of Hemingway's conversation with himself about his art, the matter of life and death.

And that is why at the end of "For Whom the Bell Tolls" (1940), Robert Jordan, a teacher turned Loyalist soldier, lies on the floor of the Spanish forest, "pulling hard on the leg, so the broken end of the bone would not come up and cut through the thigh." He is pinned in place by a leg so badly damaged that he cannot leave his post. He must delay the Fascists, who are approaching, while his comrades escape.

He loads his submachine gun, responds to the pain of his leg and tells himself, "Oh, let them come . . . I don't want to do that business that my father did. I will do it all right but I'd much prefer not to have to. I'm against that. Don't think about that." He is thinking, of course, about his father's suicide and the need to ignore his own screams because, compared to his mission, they are not important. As the pain increases, he thinks, "Maybe I'll do it now. I guess I'm not awfully good at pain." And then: "Listen, I may have to do that because if I pass out or anything like that I am no good at all and if they bring me to they will ask me a lot of questions and do things and all and that is no good. . . . So why wouldn't it be all right to just do it now and then the whole thing would be over with?"

Those doubts and fears, that pain, are the screams. Robert Jordan replies to them with "Because oh, listen, yes, listen, let them come now." He prays for rescue in action that will kill him, but that will not be self-murder. The dialectic goes on, the interior screaming, the refusal to obey the screams: "I think it would be all right to do it now? Don't you?" and then "No, it isn't. Because there is something you can do yet."

Jordan instructs himself to think not of his fear and pain but of his obligations, of his comrades' escaping, of the woman he loves, of Montana. He meditates on the wound itself. And then the desire to die interrupts: "It would be all right to do it now. Really, I'm telling you that it would be all right." But he resists, telling himself that "One thing well done can make—" and then stops. He has spoken as soldier and for Hemingway as writer.

At that moment, the enemy comes into sight, and Jordan knows that he can perform his duty and be killed in the firefight. His final sensation, in the novel's last sentence, is "his heart beating against the pine needle floor of the forest." His death announces his life.

As I have been suggesting, I see a lot of criticism as name-calling and not very useful to the understanding by readers of how literature functions or by writers of how they could be better at their trade. I have no doubt we could talk of all these shattered limbs, and add of course the missing arm of Harry Morgan, the hero of "To Have and Have Not," then call ourselves Freudian, call Hemingway emasculated or fretful about his masculinity, and then not have to read him anymore. We could talk about social guilt, call ourselves Marxists and Robert Jordan an apology by Hemingway for being a class enemy, and then not have to read him anymore. We could indicate Hemingway's androgynous women or women turned into "daughter" and discuss incest with strong mothers and sisters and clinging "daughters" and women whose haircuts make them seem like boys, and then not have to read him anymore.

This kind of dismissal, this filing away of writers in categories that trundle home like mortuary drawers, can, of course, extend to biography. We can call him a bigot and not read him. We can call him a depressive, the child of a depressive, a man who thought of suicide all his life, and then not have to read him anymore. Obviously, I am in favor of reading him to learn from his art what he clearly was compelled to say again and again: that the refusal to hear the screams and to give in to them was based on the need to perform dangerous duty, from the life-saving delivery of "Indian Camp," when death is born to a boy, to the rear-guard faithfulness of "For Whom the Bell Tolls." Each of these acts—the doctoring, the soldiering, the other activities such as bullfighting and big-game hunting that dominated Hemingway's life—was an analogue to writing because writing mattered as much as living.

When the writing went badly, he must have thought more about killing himself. When he could recover his commitment and skill, the lure of dying must have receded. He was familiar with suicide all of his life, and he wrote best about it when he created an art that served as a bulwark against it.

In the cobbled-together form of "The Garden of Eden," which Scribners published in 1986, Hemingway said of his writer protagonist:

> When he finally gave up writing that day it was afternoon. He had started a sentence as soon as he had gone into his working room and had completed it but he could write nothing after it. He crossed it out and started another sentence and again came to the complete blankness. He was unable to write the sentence that should follow although he knew it. He wrote a first simple declarative sentence again and it was impossible for him to put down the next sentence on paper. At the end of two hours it was the same. He could not write more than a single sentence and the sentences themselves were increasingly simple and completely dull. He kept at it for four hours before he knew that resolution was powerless against what had happened.

These brilliantly frightening words, icy and truthful, are about the death of narrative. Hemingway, a strong man grown frail, was finished and he knew it, saying so in the novel he had tried to write since 1946. He tolled his death as a writer with clarity and precision; such good writing about writing does not seek analogy but is starkly about the panic and "complete blankness" that terrorizes writers.

I have talked about some of the plainest and most poignant examples I know of Ernest Hemingway's dedication to his art, which was hardly selfless and priestlike, but which was— and this is my point—selfish and afraid. He did his work because it meant his life to him. His story is alive with death, and with his sense that he would inevitably reach out of it. What I have talked about is the obvious trail he left in his art of his lifelong movement between the most terrible sounds of life and the final silence with which serious writers seem somehow to be familiar.

Hemingway, like each of us, was sentenced to his life. He had been able to endure it not by way of his roistering and the action into which he entered so furiously but because of his art. He killed himself with a double-barreled shotgun because a writer's life depends on doing the writing. When that stops, the writer does too.

NOTES

1. "A Silent, Ghastly Procession," *Toronto Daily Star* (20 October 1922), reprinted in *Dateline: Toronto,* edited by William White (New York: Scribners, 1985), p. 232.

2. "Notes on the Next War: A Serious Topical Letter," *Esquire* (September 1935), reprinted in *By-Line: Ernest Hemingway,* edited by White (New York: Scribners, 1967), p. 205.

3. "Bombing of Tortosa," NANA Dispatch (15 April 1938), reprinted in *By-Line,* p. 284.

4. *A Moveable Feast* (New York: Scribners, 1964), p. 91.

5. Hemingway to Perkins (24 July 1926), in *The Only Thing That Counts: The Ernest Hemingway/Maxwell Perkins Correspondence,* edited by Matthew J. Bruccoli (Scribners, 1996), p. 43.

6. Hemingway to Perkins (21 August 1926), ibid., p. 44.

7. Hemingway to Perkins (ca. 16 November 1926), ibid., p. 48.

8. Hemingway to Perkins (11 October 1928), ibid., p. 82.

9. Hemingway to Perkins (7 June 1929), ibid., pp. 101–102.

10. Hemingway to Fitzgerald (13 September 1929), in *Ernest Hemingway: Selected Letters, 1917–1961,* edited by Carlos Baker (New York: Scribners, 1981), p. 306.

11. Hemingway to Perkins (3 October 1929), in *The Only Thing That Counts,* pp. 118–119.

12. Hemingway to Romaine (6 July 1932), in *Selected Letters,* p. 363.

13. Hemingway to Dos Passos (14 October 1932), ibid., p. 375.

14. Hemingway to Ivan Kashkin (19 August 1935), ibid., p. 419.

15. Hemingway to Perkins (30 May 1942), in *The Only Thing That Counts,* p. 318.

16. Hemingway to McCarthy (8 May 1950), in *Selected Letters,* p. 693. This letter may not have been mailed.

17. Hemingway to Perkins (13 June 1933), in *The Only Thing That Counts,* p. 190.

18. Hemingway to Rawlings (16 August 1936), in *Selected Letters,* p. 449.

19. Hemingway to Faulkner (23 July 1947), ibid., pp. 624–625.

20. Hemingway to W. G. Rogers (29 July 1948), ibid., pp. 649–650.

21. Hemingway to Fenton (18 June 1952), ibid., p. 764.

22. Hemingway to Fenton (29 July 1952), ibid., pp. 775–777.

HEMINGWAY AS STUDIED

OVERVIEW

One of the most common misconceptions about Ernest Hemingway is to assume that as only a high-school graduate, he was not particularly well educated or well read. True, he never attended a university, but he educated himself far beyond what he would have learned in the classroom. By the time he died, his library in Cuba held more than eight thousand volumes. He was well read on European history, military tactics, World War I, the American Civil War, the American West, Italy, Spain, East Africa, fishing and hunting, and contemporary writers. He spoke with varying degrees of fluency French, Spanish, Italian, German, and a little Swahili. He was an astute analyst of politics, an avid and continuous traveler, a reader of poetry, and was well schooled in classical music. His public image of outdoorsman, brawler, and drinker was a comfortable mask that protected the sensitive, hard-working professional writer.

Hemingway's most obvious links to earlier writers can be found in his several lists of books that would-be authors should read and in his list of his own literary forebears. Whether or not any of these authors actually influenced Hemingway's development is a question still in the process of reaching resolution, but his lists do tell something about Hemingway and the era in which he matured. For example, the 1935 list has only one living author on it: James Joyce, whom Hemingway knew during the Paris years. The rest are all from the nineteenth century and earlier, and almost all are British or European, for these literatures dominated the classrooms of America well into the twentieth century. Until the mid 1930s one could not get a graduate degree in American literature. The modernist generation, to which Hemingway was a late admission, looked very new at the time. International in background, the modernists set the compass marks for the twentieth century's writers, painters, and musicians. But they were also the last generation to honor the nineteenth century. Like all of the modernists, Hemingway's admitted literary roots were in the past. In Oak Park he read British authors; in

Summer, 1959. Hemingway, weary from road travel back and forth across Spain, stands beside his newfound idol, matador Antonio Ordóñez, dressed in his "suit of lights" and preparing to face the fighting bull that awaits him in the sandy ring. The son of Cayetano Ordóñez, who was the model for Pedro Romero in *The Sun Also Rises*, Antonio was engaged in an extended series of *mano-a-mano* competitions with the older matador Luis Dominguín.

Paris he read the French and Russian authors. Writing a note to himself, he once said that the point of reading was to find an author obscure enough that one might steal from him without others recognizing it. He also said that a writer must pay nominal dues to the past because he needed to know what had been written so well that it need not be done again. It was only with the great dead writers that one competed.

But Hemingway's lists do not tell us all we need to know about writers who influenced his art, for his lists are partial, selections made to reinforce the public image he created. There are many unlisted nineteenth-century writers whose veiled presence can be felt in Hemingway's fiction. In *Hemingway's Quarrel With Androgyny* Mark Spilka has done a remarkable job of tracing out some of these influences. One also notes that Hemingway has said nothing about his several contemporaries from whom he learned: Sherwood Anderson, Ezra Pound, Gertrude Stein, F. Scott Fitzgerald, T. S. Eliot, and William Faulkner. Nor does he admit Jack London to the list, an author he read and imitated early. In his 1916 high-school notebook, Hemingway set down a far shorter and less self-conscious list: O. Henry, Rudyard Kipling, and Stewart Edward White. Do not suppose that he left these writers behind when he sailed to Europe. Kipling appears in several unexpected places, for example in "The Brushwood Boy" and in *A Farewell to Arms*. And O. Henry's patented twist at the end of the story shows up in "The Short Happy Life of Francis Macomber" and "The Snows of Kilimanjaro," both of which are among Hemingway's most-read stories.

When one examines Hemingway's reading between 1910 and 1940, he finds that biography, literary history, novels, and travel books dominated his library. When he found an author he liked, he tended to read everything by that author he could find. After high school and before Paris, he read several volumes of Joseph Conrad's, including *The Rover* (1923), *Typhoon* (1902), and *Victory* (1915). Sherwood Anderson's *Winesburg, Ohio* (1919) impressed the young Hemingway sufficiently that one of his first mature short stories, "My Old Man," is written in Anderson's voice. In Paris, besides absorbing Continental authors, Hemingway learned most about modernist fiction from James Joyce and Gertrude Stein. Read *Dubliners* side by side with *In Our Time* to feel the Joycean technique at work, particularly the way the stories end. To see what he learned from Stein, read any of her experimental sketches alongside Hemingway's "Mr. and Mrs. Elliot," which is consciously written in Stein's voice. Having read Fitzgerald's *The Great Gatsby* shortly before he began *The Sun Also Rises*, Hemingway created conscious parallels between the two novels.

THE WAR NOVEL

A Farewell to Arms is now remembered as *the* American war novel from World War I. Coming, as it did, eleven years after that war's end, it was preceded by a small library of war novels, histories, and memoirs, few of which survived their immediate readership. Only two other war novels from that period have had a lasting impact on the genre. In 1929, Erich Maria Remarque's *Im Westen nichts Neues* was published, along with an English translation, *All Quiet on the Western Front;* and in 1935 Humphrey Cobb's *Paths of Glory* was published. Comparisons between these two and Hemingway's novel are particularly interesting for what *A Farewell to Arms* does and does not do. For example, both Remarque and Cobb give grim, extended, and detailed descriptions of the trench warfare that drained the blood and the morale of millions of soldiers. Hemingway shows very little of the war at first hand; it is always there, haunting the characters, but the reader feels it more than he sees it. What is lacking in Cobb and Remarque and what Hemingway gives to the war novel is the love interest between Frederic and Catherine. Critics argued long and late about whether *A Farewell to Arms* was a love story set in war, or a war story played out against the background of romance, but their either/or debates were largely pointless. After 1929, the war novel came in two varieties: the traditional all-male cast engaged in the gritty actuality of war, and the lovers caught up in a war that determines their fates. Hemingway combined both structures in *A Farewell to Arms,* and later in *The Fifth Column, For Whom the Bell Tolls,* and *Across the River and into the Trees.* James Jones would use this combination in *From Here to Eternity,* and Hollywood movies would use it over and over again between 1940 and 1950.

A Farewell to Arms became the model for many twentieth-century war stories, but it was not the first war story to have a love interest. One need look no further than Homer's *Iliad,* Tolstoy's *War and Peace* (1865–1869), or Stendhal's *The Charterhouse of Parma* (1839) to find examples with which Hemingway was quite familiar. Nor was the Hemingway novel the first great American war novel; that accolade goes to Stephen Crane's *The Red Badge of Courage* (1895), a book with which *A Farewell to Arms* is sometimes compared. In Paris, Hemingway learned from Ford Madox Ford that Crane, who had never been to the American Civil War, wrote the book from research. Hemingway, who saw little of the war in Italy, researched the retreat from Caporetto so well that Italians who had

been there were certain he had also participated in that debacle. Hemingway also used Stendhal's account in *The Charterhouse of Parma* of the retreat from Waterloo as a model, resulting in interesting comparisons.

In his subsequent war novels, Hemingway again mixed firsthand experience with his reading to produce remarkably accurate fiction. *For Whom the Bell Tolls,* for example, draws on Hemingway's experience as a journalist in the Spanish Civil War, but it also uses T. E. Lawrence's vivid descriptions of guerrilla warfare in his memoir *Revolt in the Desert* (1927), a book Hemingway owned and read in 1931. Both Lawrence and Jordan are fluent in local dialects, know the terrain from prewar travel, and are adept in the customs of the country. Robert Jordan's fictional background as a saboteur, including the mercy killing of his accomplice, comes right out of Lawrence's adventures blowing up trains in Arabia. When Lawrence's Arab friend Farraj cannot be abandoned to the Turks, Lawrence is forced to shoot him just as Jordan is forced to shoot his friend Kashkin. *For Whom the Bell Tolls* also bears an interesting structural comparison with *The Iliad.* Both stories make ample use of epic conventions to enrich their narratives. For example, the rescue of Maria, El Sordo's hilltop fight, the story of Maria's rape, and Pilar's story of the first day of the revolution are all epic digressions.

Today most war novelists agree that no one can write a *For Whom the Bell Tolls* again. As Vietnam veteran and war novelist Tim O'Brien has said, if a war story makes you feel good, you may be certain that it was not based on a true story. But O'Brien and most of his contemporaries would freely admit that Hemingway provided the voice, the tone, and the detachment that was like a gift to their generation of writers. If they find it impossible to create love-and-war fiction, they have other Hemingway models to draw on: "A Natural History of the Dead," "A Way You'll Never Be," "Now I Lay Me," "Soldier's Home," and those early vignettes in which Nick is up against the wall, literally and figuratively. Hemingway's influence can be seen in O'Brien's *The Things They Carried* (1990), where Hemingway's voice is there beneath the flow.

"*For Whom the Bell Tolls* is nothing to warrant a display of adjectives. Adjectives are dug from soil too long worked, and they make sickly praise and stumbling reading. I think that what you do about this book of Ernest Hemingway's is point to it and say, 'Here is a book.' As you would stand below Everest and say, 'Here is a mountain.'"

Dorothy Parker

From "Mr. Hemingway's Finest Story Yet," *PM* (20 October 1940): 42.

THE AMERICAN-IN-EUROPE THEME

Ketchum, Idaho, January 1961. His eyes vacant from the first series of electroshock treatments at the Mayo Clinic, Hemingway holds his shotgun, the breech broken. Suffering from depression, paranoia, insomnia, and diabetes, he is noticeably gaunt. Within six weeks, after attempts to kill himself, he returned to the Mayo for more shock treatments, which did not relieve his depression. Five months after this picture was taken, Hemingway put an end to his life.

Growing up as he did almost bereft of his American literary heritage, Hemingway arrived in Paris in 1921 not having read Henry James. That deficiency was soon remedied by the reading advice he received from all sides. His wife, Hadley, was a devotee of James novels; Gertrude Stein told him to read James, as did Ezra Pound, who specifically advised him to read *The American* (1877) and *Portrait of a Lady* (1881) among other works. In 1924, Ford Madox Ford regaled him with stories about James. When Hemingway was awarded the Nobel Prize in literature, he regretted, he said, that Mark Twain and Henry James had never received the award. His library at La Finca Vigía outside of Havana held nine of James's books. Like James, Hemingway explored the theme of the American in Europe extensively, but to different ends. James's somewhat naive American visitors to England or the Continent are frequently taken advantage of by more subtle, sophisticated, and devious Europeans, and his Americans who have lived as expatriates in Europe lose touch with their native land. Hemingway's Americans abroad travel in a postwar Europe where fine titles and noble heritage have lost most of their meaning. James's *Daisy Miller* (1878) and Hemingway's "A Canary For One" are different versions of a similar story, and Hemingway's story contains specific references to *Daisy Miller*. James's *The Aspern Papers* (1888) serves as background for *Across the River and into the Trees*. Hemingway's characters in *The Garden of Eden* become as corrupted as any of James's characters too long in Europe. Like James, like Conrad, Hemingway frequently isolates his Americans in another country to test their moral values without benefit of a supporting culture.

THE COMING-OF-AGE STORY

Speaking for himself, Hemingway once said that American literature began with *Huck Finn*—an oversimplification but in some ways true for Hemingway. His earliest stories from *In Our Time* tell of a young boy, Nick Adams, coming of age in northern Michigan. Like Huck, Nick learns early about fear and death in "Indian Camp," where violent birth is eclipsed by the Indian father's suicide. Afterward, rowing back across the lake, Nick asks his father, the Doctor, if dying is hard. Like Huck, Nick has problems with his father. Huck in the cabin ready to kill his drunken father with the shotgun reappears in "Fathers and Sons" where Nick Adams, sitting in the woodshed with his loaded shotgun, watches his father and thinks how easy it would be to kill him. Like Huck, Nick learns almost everything the hard way through experience. Nick's encounter with the punch-drunk Ad Francis in "The Battler" echoes the violence and the untrustworthy adults Huck meets on his trip downriver. Late in his career, when Hemingway returned to Nick and his sister Littless in "The Last Good Country," the ghosts of Huck and Tom lurk on the periphery of Hemingway's story. With both authors, the effects of violence on their young characters are more important than the violence itself. Huck, who refuses to tell everything that happened at the Grangerfords, says that he has bad dreams from the killings. Nick, lying awake at night listening to the silkworms munching ("Now I Lay Me"), has difficulty sleeping as a result of violence sustained.

"...the lad in the Rue de Notre Dame des Champs

In the carpenter's loft on the left-hand side going down—

The lad with the supple look like a sleepy panther—

And what became of him? Fame became of him.

Veteran out of the wars before he was twenty:

Famous at twenty-five: thirty a master—

Whittled a style for his time from a walnut stick

In a carpenter's loft in a street of that April city."

Archibald MacLeish

From "HIS MIRROR WAS DANGER," *Life*, 51 (14 July 1961): 70–71.

Another interesting comparison can be made between the Nick Adams stories and J. D. Salinger's *Catcher in the Rye* (1951). Holden Caulfield, like his blood brothers Huck and Nick, has no love for the adult world, which both frightens and repulses him. The knowledge of death, from which adults try to shield their children, haunts all three boys. On the river, the dead bodies pile up, and Huck witnesses his own funeral. For Holden there is the knowledge of his brother's death and the fear of becoming an adult. At the end, all three carry psychic wounds that leave them on the margin of life. Huck intends to "light out" for the territories before someone else tries to civilize him, saying he has been there before. Holden tries to make the same escape but fails. At the end of his story, he is on the psychiatrist's couch, reminding the reader of Nick Adams in "A Way You'll Never Be," telling Paravicini that once a man has

"Well, I guess some of us write and some of us pitch, but so far there isn't any law a man has to go and see *The Cocktail Party*, by T. S. Eliot from St. Louis, where Yogi Berra comes from. A damned good poet and a fair critic, but he would not have existed except for dear old Ezra [Pound], the lovely poet and stupid traitor."

Ernest Hemingway

From Harvey Breit, "Talk with Mr. Hemingway," *New York Times Book Review,* 17 September 1950, p. 14.

been certified crazy no one has faith in him again. In the last story in which Nick appears, "Fathers and Sons," Nick is driving west, unable to explain to his son anything significant about his grandfather or how the Indians were when Nick was a boy.

HEMINGWAY AND WRITERS OF THE 1920S

The three writers of the 1920s with whom Hemingway is most often associated are Ezra Pound, Gertrude Stein, and F. Scott Fitzgerald. Of the three, Pound may be the most important influence on Hemingway's development, but Stein receives more critical attention. From all three Hemingway received invaluable advice, criticism, and professional help when he most needed it. Pound's advice on whom to read was most valuable to Hemingway's education as a writer. Pound advocated what he and Eliot called the Tradition: Homer, Catullus, Ovid, Geoffrey Chaucer, Dante, François Villon, and John Donne, all of whom would appear in Hemingway's future work. The irascible poet sent Hemingway to Henry James, Gustave Flaubert, and Stendhal, writers vital to Hemingway's development. It was Pound who first told him that all great writers draw on other great writers from the past as Eliot did in *The Waste Land* (1922) and as Joyce did in *Ulysses*. One should either acknowledge his debt or conceal it. It was Pound who told Hemingway that symbols must first occur as natural objects in the fiction, or as Hemingway would say later, symbols were not like raisins to be stuck into the bread dough. Equally important were the concepts of Imagism that Pound drilled into young Hemingway while critiquing his apprentice writing. Treat the thing itself, Pound told him. Avoid as many adjectives as possible. Good art is precise art, bearing true witness. Eliminate, eliminate. By the time Hemingway had absorbed what Pound had to teach him, he had perfected his own version of simplicity, understatement, and irony, the results of which he called "the way it was."

What Hemingway learned from Stein was less programmatic, but no less useful. Through his semiregular attendance at Stein's salon, Hemingway made contact with the postimpressionist and modernist painters who influenced his early work, teaching him about landscape, color, and telling detail. After digesting Stein's *Three Lives* (1909), Hemingway also took a short course in reading Stein's experimental writing, which he said was an excellent method for taking notes. Looking through his unpublished exercises written during the 1922–1924 Paris period, one can find his Steinesque imitations, which culminate in his story "Mr. and Mrs. Elliot." In 1924, while working on Ford Madox Ford's *transatlantic review,* Hemingway transcribed large portions of Stein's *The Making of Americans* into setting copy for the periodical. Stein's influence can be traced through most of Hemingway's 1920s writing, in which he took from her what he could use and made it more accessible than she was able to do at the time.

The relationship between Hemingway and F. Scott Fitzgerald is more complicated and twisted than any of his other literary friendships from the 1920s. The most authoritative history of their friendship is Matthew J. Bruccoli's *Fitzgerald and Hemingway: A Dangerous Friendship* (New York: Carroll & Graf, 1994). Both writers were aware of each other before they ever met. Hemingway first read Fitzgerald's *This Side of Paradise* (1920) in 1921 when he was still in Chicago writing bad imitations of popular fiction. His wife-to-be, Hadley, commenting on Hemingway's first attempt at a novel, suggested that the narrative flow was too disrupted, as they had noted about Fitzgerald's novel. When Scott and Ernest finally met in 1925, Fitzgerald had just published *The Great Gatsby,* which Ernest read before going to Spain that summer. After the unpleasantness of Pamplona in mid July, when he nearly came to blows with Harold Loeb over Duff Twysden, Hemingway began writing *The Sun Also Rises,* which bears interesting parallels with *The Great Gatsby:* the woman around whom the men circle; the narrator trying to understand the import of his story; the failure of values; the loss of idealism. The two novels became and continue to be important historical data points, signals that something has gone seriously wrong with the moral standards of the times.

RESOURCES FOR
HEMINGWAY STUDY

STUDY QUESTIONS

1. Compare any of Hemingway's journalistic accounts of public events with coverage from your local newspaper or with the memories of someone in town who was present at the event. For example, use Hemingway's account of the D-day landing on Omaha Beach, "Voyage to Victory," in *By-Line: Ernest Hemingway*.

2. Use the same Hemingway feature story about the Fox Green sector of Omaha Beach and compare it with the way it was filmed in Steven Spielberg's 1998 movie *Saving Private Ryan*. What are the similarities and differences?

3. For any event in Hemingway's life or fiction, look through your local newspaper to see how it was treated. For example, use the retreat from Caporetto in *A Farewell to Arms*; or, in *For Whom the Bell Tolls*, Pilar's account of the atrocities committed on the first day of the Spanish Civil War.

4. Read Hemingway's "Soldier's Home," and interview any local war veteran to see if his or her experience resembles that of Hemingway's returning soldier.

5. Choose one of the following Hemingway stories to stage as reader's theater: "Hills Like White Elephants," "The End of Something," "A Clean, Well-Lighted Place," or "Ten Indians." Be sure to include a narrator in the cast. Discuss afterward what was learned from hearing the story that was not apparent when reading it. Using the assessments in the "Aftershocks" section of chapter 5, see if what the critics said about Hemingway's inability to write convincingly about male/female relationships fits your experience with the story.

6. Look at the way a Hemingway short story begins. Compare his opening paragraph with those of other writers you have read. What are the similarities and differences?

7. Watch the 1958 movie *The Old Man and the Sea*. Compare what you see with the novel you have read. Which is more convincing, more interesting? Why?

8. Using a 1:250,000 scale map of northern Italy, trace out the action from *A Farewell to Arms*.

9. Using a Paris street map and a map of northern Spain, do the same for *The Sun Also Rises*. These maps can probably be found on the Internet if they are not available locally.

10. Draw a map that depicts the setting described in "Hills Like White Elephants." What does it tell you about the central issue of the story? Does this work for any other Hemingway short stories?

11. From books on the history of art, find a definition of landscape painting. Then look at the landscapes described in *A Farewell to Arms, The Sun Also Rises, Green Hills of Africa,* or "Big Two-Hearted River." How do Hemingway's written landscapes compare with painted landscapes?

12. Read "A Canary for One" and Henry James's *Daisy Miller*. What conclusions can be made about the relationship between the two stories? Why does Hemingway make veiled references to the James story?

13. Read "My Old Man" and one of Sherwood Anderson's racetrack stories. How are they similar? How are they different? Or do the same for Hemingway's "Mr. and Mrs. Elliot" and Gertrude Stein's "Melanctha" section from *Three Lives*.

14. Find the useful Internet sites with Hemingway information. What kinds of sites are out there? Which are the most helpful in reading Hemingway?

GLOSSARY OF LITERARY TERMS*

Abstraction: In common usage, abstract refers to language whose meaning is imprecisely expressed. In modernist art, it has a more positive connotation. Through abstraction, a writer suggests the general characteristics of the subject matter by depicting its particulars in a new, provocative way.

Aesthetics: Formally, aesthetics is a branch of philosophy concerned with defining elemental aspects of beauty. Informally, in literary criticism the term is used to designate the qualities of art valued by a specific author or literary movement.

Allusion: An allusion is a reference to a literary work, character, or setting. It is used to suggest unexpressed significance that a reader may or may not perceive, depending upon his or her knowledge of myth, history, and literature. Allusions allowed modernist writers to establish a connection to the past in their poetry and fiction.

Ambiguity: Not unlike abstraction, ambiguous ordinarily means unclear or unspecific. As a literary technique, however, ambiguity often reflects a writer's desire to convey the complexity of the moral or psychological conflict of a work without oversimplification. For example, Jake Barnes's dilemma in *The Sun Also Rises* can be described as ambiguous because Hemingway never explicitly explains Jake's motives for

* Adapted from Kirk Curnutt's Gale Study Guide, *Ernest Hemingway and the Expatriate Modernist Movement*

introducing Brett Ashley to Pedro Romero. Does he facilitate their affair because he genuinely wants Brett to be happy, or is he perversely punishing himself for his own inability to love her? While ambiguity can be frustrating for readers, it can also be liberating in allowing them to explore their own responses to events in a story.

Archetype: An archetype is a character, theme, image, or event common to a broad array of cultures and social groups. Adam and Eve's expulsion from the Garden of Eden can be considered archetypal, for instance, since similar stories of humanity's fall from grace and initiation into evil are found in religions other than Christianity. Modernists often employed archetypes in the same way they used allusions—to heighten the mythic aspect of their writings and connect them with ancient traditions.

Compression: Compression is a writing technique that avoids explaining or elaborating upon the significance of a character or event, suggesting it instead through a symbol or image. Hemingway's style in *In Our Time* can be considered compressed because his sentences are generally short, descriptive, and devoid of unnecessary words. See also *Iceberg Principle*.

Cubism: Cubism is a style of modernist painting (ca. 1907–1915) led by Pablo Picasso and Georges Braque in which forms are broken down into geometric shapes. Its earliest phase (called "analytical cubism") juxtaposed these shapes, creating the illusion of viewing an object from many angles simultaneously. In its later, post-1912 stage ("synthetic cubism") artists incorporated pieces of newspaper and fabric into the composition, creating a collage effect. One modernist text that aims to translate Cubists' visual techniques into writing is Gertrude Stein's *Tender Buttons* (1914).

Decadence: Normally, decadence refers to behavior that violates the mores of a culture by indulging an individual's desire for gratification. Thus, promiscuity is considered decadent because it disregards social standards of monogamy for the self's craving for physical pleasure. In the late nineteenth century, a literary genre known as the decadent movement arose; it condoned deviancy as a way to achieve individual enlightenment. It also encouraged its members to explore the effects of drugs and sexual taboos in their writing. By the 1920s, decadent was a common synonym for the expatriate movement, although only a handful of modernists openly believed in stimulating the imagination through artificial means.

Dramatis Personae: This term refers to the cast of characters in a play and, by extension, in other fictional works.

Exile: As opposed to expatriate, exile connotes banishment from one's homeland, usually for political or moral reasons.

Expatriation: Expatriation is the act of voluntarily living outside of one's native country.

Fragmentation: Fragmentation is a literary technique by which modernists broke down a story or plot into a single episode or image. Traditionally, a narrative is supposed to possess unity, meaning it progresses from a beginning to a middle to an ending resolution. Modernists, however, often flashed upon individual moments of significance without supplying background, character development, or a conclusion. The vignettes in Hemingway's *In Our Time* can be considered examples of fragments—they fix upon a moment of violence without explaining what happened before or after it. T. S. Eliot in *The Waste Land* employs a different sort of fragmentation: he shifts scenes, speakers, and settings without cuing readers or explaining their transitions. For modernists, fragmentation was a way of conveying the sense that modern life possessed little continuity with the past.

Genre: Genre is a French term describing categories of literature. Poetry is a genre, as are the novel and the short story. A genre is often the result of an effort to classify different types of writing, distinguishing them by the characteristics unique to their class. Definitions of genres are always changing, however, as critics challenge and revise previous scholars' descriptions of the traits of various categories.

Harlem Renaissance: This term describes a movement of African-American writers in the 1920s to expand the possibilities of black writing in America. Writers such as Langston Hughes, Claude McKay, Nella Larsen, and Zora Neale Hurston described the varieties of life in African-American urban communities. They often blended folkloric tales and styles with modernist techniques borrowed from James Joyce, T. S. Eliot, and Ezra Pound. The movement was seen as a renaissance or rebirth because its authors were celebrating black communities rather than defending them from racist attacks or protesting prejudices. Although the movement identified Harlem as its central site, several writers—including Hughes, McKay, and Countee Cullen—also visited Paris for brief periods of time in the 1920s.

Iceberg Principle: This phrase is commonly used among critics to describe Hemingway's style of omission. In *Death in the Afternoon*, Hemingway writes: "If a writer of prose knows enough about what he is writing about he may omit things that he knows and the reader, if the writer is writing truly enough, will have a feeling of those things as strongly as though the writer had stated them. The dignity of movement of an iceberg is due to only one-eighth of it being above water." A good example of Hemingway's omission is the absence of the word *abortion* in "Hills Like White Elephants."

Imagism: Ezra Pound announced the birth of this school of modern poetry in 1912. Its principal aim was to avoid the excess verbiage that marred contemporary verse. It also conveyed intense emotions through a concentrated description of an object. The quintessential imagist poem is Pound's "In the Station of the Metro," which reads in its entirety: "The apparition of these faces in the crowd, / Petals on a wet, black bough." Pound eventually abandoned Imagism out of annoyance with American poet Amy Lowell, who became the school's chief public spokeswoman. Something of Imagism's intense brevity can be found in Hemingway's terse style, which Pound encouraged.

Initiation Story: Also known as the "coming-of-age" tale, initiation story refers to a type of plot in which an adolescent recognizes the moral complexity of adulthood, either by failing his/her own value system or by observing the hypocrisy of an adult authority.

Juxtaposition: Juxtaposition is a modernist technique of contrast by which two different elements of a painting or poem are set next to each other, thus emphasizing the differences. Eliot's *The Waste Land* offers several examples, such as when the poem opposes fragments of modern discourse to excerpts from classical and Renaissance literature.

Metaphor: A figure of speech by which a single word or a phrase dramatizes the qualities of another object or emotion, metaphors differ from similes in that the similes assert a similarity between two things, marked by "such as" or "like," whereas with metaphors the relationship between the two terms is implied. Thus, "love is a rose" is a metaphor, while "love is like a rose" is a simile.

Métier: One of Gertrude Stein's favorite terms, this French word refers to a genre, form, or activity to which someone's talents are well suited. Thus, writing was Hemingway's métier, while painting was Pablo Picasso's.

Modernism: A broad term that describes movements in the arts from roughly 1900 to the end of World War II. In literature, the adjective *modernist* is typically applied to works of this era that are complex and experimental, that strive to present new ways of describing perception and consciousness, and that are pessimistic about human evolution and progress. There are many subcategories of modernism—including futurism, cubism, and Vorticism—to name but three. The term "high modernism" is also used frequently to distinguish the most technically dense and difficult modernist works, including James Joyce's *Ulysses* and T. S. Eliot's *The Waste Land.*

Postimpressionism: This term in the 1890s and early 1900s described the generation of painters who rebelled against impressionism. Postimpressionists preferred sharper outlines and bolder colors than their predecessors. Of this group, Paul Cézanne was the most influential among modernists.

Primitivism: Primitivism is a rebellious tendency in the arts to break from rules and prescriptions for what Western art should be to explore sensuous (and sensual) emotions. Modernists cultivated primitive techniques as a result of their fascination with African culture. Because Europeans and Americans considered African cultures "uncultivated," they viewed their various forms of artistic expression as more spontaneous and authentic than approaches learned through formal training.

Roman à clef: Literally, this French phrase means "novel with a key." The term refers to narratives in which fictional characters are modeled on real-life people whom readers are meant to recognize. *The Sun Also Rises* is a roman à clef because Hemingway based Brett Ashley, Mike Campbell, Bill Gorton, and others in the novel on Parisian friends and acquaintances, including Duff Twysden, Pat Guthrie, and Donald Ogden Stewart, respectively.

Stream of consciousness: Originally coined by Gertrude Stein's teacher William James (philosopher brother of novelist Henry James), stream of consciousness is a literary technique that presents a character's perceptions as a rush of sensations rather than as an orderly arrangement of ideas. James Joyce popularized the use of this device in *Ulysses;* other famous examples include Virginia Woolf's *Mrs. Dalloway* (1925) and William Faulkner's *The Sound and the Fury* (1929). Hemingway experimented with stream of consciousness, most effectively in the passages detailing Harry's memories in "The Snows of Kilimanjaro." With the exception of his use of stream of consciousness in this story, the technique is not considered his strength.

Surrealism: Meaning "superrealism," this term describes a literary movement that arose from disagreements among Dadaists in the mid 1920s. Surrealist writers such as André Breton and Louis Aragon and painters such as Man Ray aimed to tap into the creative resources of the unconscious mind with dreamlike visions of unconventional images.

Symbol: A symbol is an object or action that stands for an idea. Thus, in "The Snows of Kilimanjaro," both the snow and the mountain symbolize different aspects of Harry's life and personality as he prepares for death—though just what those aspects are largely depends upon the reader's interpretation.

Vorticism: Ezra Pound and Wyndham Lewis founded this avant-garde school of modernism in the 1910s. Vorticists rebelled against genteel nineteenth-century poetry and art, insisting that modern works must acknowledge the effects of technology, violence, and dynamic motion in their work. Julian Symons explains that the central image of the movement, the vortex, reflected a desire to establish art as "the still point of maximum energy in the midst of conflicting forces, as there is said to be stillness at the heart of a whirlpool." In other words, art and literature should not only reflect the chaos of cultural change but also should be a catalytic force in shaping its future.

BIBLIOGRAPHY

BASIC REFERENCE WORKS

Brasch, James, and Joseph Sigmund. *Hemingway's Library.* New York: Garland, 1981. Necessary to any source study of Hemingway's post-1940 writing.

Catalog of the Ernest Hemingway Collection at the John F. Kennedy Library, 2 volumes. Boston: G. K. Hall, 1982.

Hanneman, Audre. *Ernest Hemingway, A Comprehensive Bibliography,* 2 volumes. Princeton: Princeton University Press, 1967; supplement, 1975. Vital research tool.

Larson, Kelli. *Ernest Hemingway: A Reference Guide, 1974–1989.* Boston: G. K. Hall, 1991.

Mandel, Miriam B. *Reading Hemingway: The Facts in the Fiction.* Metuchen, N.J.: Scarecrow Press, 1995. Excellent resource for references in the works.

Oliver, Charles. *Ernest Hemingway A to Z.* New York: Facts on File, 1999.

Reynolds, Michael. *Hemingway's Reading 1910–1940.* Princeton: Princeton University Press, 1981. Also available on-line at the Hemingway Collection home page, John F. Kennedy Library (http://www.cs.umb.edu/jfklibrary/index.htm).

Smith, Paul. *A Reader's Guide to the Short Stories of Ernest Hemingway.* Boston: G. K. Hall, 1989. Best single source on the creation and criticism of Hemingway's short fiction.

Waldhorn, Arthur. *A Reader's Guide to Ernest Hemingway.* New York: Farrar, Straus & Giroux, 1981.

LIBRARY COLLECTIONS

The following libraries have Hemingway collections, their most significant, but by no means their only, holdings noted in parentheses.

Blaine County Library, Ketchum, Idaho (oral histories, photographs).

Indiana University, The Lilly Library (Letters, Ezra Pound and William Bird papers).

John F. Kennedy Library, Boston (the major Hemingway collection of manuscripts, letters, secondary materials, maps, and photographs, established by Mary Hemingway).

Monroe County Library, Key West, Florida (some galleys, photographs, local history).

Oak Park Public Library, Oak Park, Illinois (*Tabula* and *Trapeze* from Oak Park High School, local newspaper, photographs).

Princeton University Library (Carlos Baker files, Scribner Author files, Patrick Hemingway Collection).

Stanford University Library (Pauline Hemingway's 1933–1934 safari journal and Hemingway-Carlos Baker correspondence).

University of Delaware Library (Cut opening of *The Sun Also Rises,* letters).

University of South Carolina, Thomas Cooper Library (Hemingway and Fitzgerald materials).

University of Texas, Humanities Research Center (*Death in the Afternoon* and parts of "Big Two-Hearted River" manuscripts, family letters).

University of Tulsa Library (some Spanish Civil War materials).

University of Virginia, Alderman Library (*Green Hills of Africa* manuscript).

Yale University, Beinecke Library (Charles Fenton Collection, letters to Gertrude Stein).

FAMILY MEMOIRS

Gellhorn, Martha. *Travels With Myself and Another.* London: Eland Books, 1983. Best source for story of Hemingway in China in 1941.

Hemingway, Gregory. *Papa.* Boston: Houghton Mifflin, 1976.

Hemingway, Jack. *Misadventures of a Fly Fisherman.* Dallas: Taylor, 1986.

Hemingway, Leicester. *My Brother, Ernest Hemingway.* Cleveland: World, 1962; revised edition, with family letters, Sarasota, Fla.: Pineapple Press, 1996.

Hemingway, Mary. *How It Was.* New York: Knopf, 1976. Based on journals she kept during their marriage.

Miller, Madelaine Hemingway. *Ernie.* New York: Crown, 1975. Best view of life in Oak Park.

Sanford, Marcelline Hemingway. *At the Hemingways.* Boston: Little, Brown, 1962; revised edition, with family letters and new introductions, Moscow: University of Idaho Press, 1999.

MEMOIRS OF OTHERS WHO KNEW HEMINGWAY

Beach, Sylvia. *Shakespeare and Company.* New York: Harcourt, Brace, 1959. Factually flawed, but a well-meaning view of Paris in the 1920s.

Brian, Denis. *The True Gen.* New York: Grove, 1988. Invaluable collection of brief takes on Hemingway.

Callaghan, Morley. *That Summer in Paris: Memories of Tangled Friendships with Hemingway, Fitzgerald, and Some Others.* New York: Coward-McCann, 1963.

Castillo-Puche, José Luis. *Hemingway in Spain,* translated by Helen R. Lane. Garden City, N.Y.: Doubleday, 1974.

Donnelly, Honoria Murphy. *Sara & Gerald: Memories of the Murphys and Their Friends.* New York: Times Books, 1982.

Loeb, Harold. *The Way It Was.* New York: Criterion Books, 1959. The prototype for Cohn in *The Sun Also Rises* tries to set the record straight.

MacLeish, Archibald. *Reflections,* edited by Bernard Drabeck and Helen Ellis. Amherst: University of Massachusetts Press, 1986.

McAlmon, Robert. *Being Geniuses Together, 1920–1930,* revised by Kay Boyle. Garden City, N.Y.: Doubleday, 1968. Biased, a little bitter, but an interesting memoir.

Ross, Lillian. *Portrait of Hemingway.* New York: Simon & Schuster, 1961. Infamous portrayal of Hemingway on a New York visit.

Samuelson, Arnold. *With Hemingway: A Year in Key West and Cuba.* New York: Random House, 1984.

Stein, Gertrude. *The Autobiography of Alice B. Toklas.* New York: Harcourt, Brace, 1933. Stein's biased view of Hemingway.

Viertel, Peter. *Dangerous Friends: At Large with Hemingway and Huston in the Fifties.* Garden City, N.Y.: Doubleday, 1992. Good take on Hemingway in the 1950s based on new letters and personal contact.

COLLECTIONS OF INTERVIEWS

The following books are compilations of interviews with those who knew Hemingway at different points in his life.

Fuentes, Noberto. *Hemingway in Cuba,* translated by Consuelo E. Corwin. Secaucus, N.J.: Lyle Stuart, 1984. Useful inside information on the Cuban years.

Paporov, Uri. *Hemingway en Cuba,* translated by Armando Partida Tayzan. Mexico City: Siglo XXI Editores, 1993. Interesting book based on interviews shortly after Hemingway's death.

Plath, James, and Frank Simons. *Remembering Ernest Hemingway.* Key West, Fla.: Ketch & Yawl Press, 1999. Wide-ranging interviews with Hemingway friends.

HEMINGWAY BIOGRAPHIES

Baker, Carlos. *Ernest Hemingway: A Life Story.* New York: Scribners, 1969. Baker's biography remains the standard one-volume life of Hemingway.

Bruccoli, Matthew J. *Fitzgerald and Hemingway: A Dangerous Friendship.* New York: Carroll & Graf, 1994. Best analysis of the famed friendship.

Donaldson, Scott. *By Force of Will: The Life and Art of Ernest Hemingway.* New York: Viking, 1977.

Fenton, Charles. *The Apprenticeship of Ernest Hemingway.* New York: Viking, 1954.

Griffin, Peter. *Along With Youth: Hemingway, the Early Years.* New York: Oxford University Press, 1985. The only source of several pre-Paris short stories.

Kert, Bernice. *The Hemingway Women.* New York: Norton, 1983. After Baker, this book is the best single-volume biography, interviews with women who would not talk to the male biographers.

Lynn, Kenneth S. *Hemingway.* New York: Simon & Schuster, 1987.

McLendon, James. *Papa: Hemingway in Key West,* revised edition. Key West, Fla.: Langley Press, 1990.

Mellow, James R. *Hemingway: A Life Without Consequences.* New York: Houghton Mifflin, 1992.

Meyers, Jeffrey. *Hemingway.* New York: Harper & Row, 1985.

Montgomery, Constance C. *Hemingway in Michigan.* New York: Fleet, 1966. Lots of local information on the Michigan lakes and woods of Hemingway's youth.

Reynolds, Michael. *Young Hemingway.* Oxford: Blackwell, 1986; New York: Norton, 1998.

Reynolds. *Hemingway: The Paris Years.* Oxford: Blackwell, 1989; New York: Norton, 1999.

Reynolds. *Hemingway: The Homecoming.* Oxford: Blackwell, 1992; New York: Norton, 1999.

Reynolds. *Hemingway: The 1930s.* New York: Norton, 1997.

Reynolds. *Hemingway: The Final Years.* New York: Norton, 1999.

OTHER BIOGRAPHIES AND HISTORIES

Benstock, Shari. *Women of the Left Bank.* Austin: University of Texas Press, 1986. A comprehensive survey. Information not easily found elsewhere.

Berg, A. Scott. *Max Perkins, Editor of Genius.* New York: E. P. Dutton, 1978. Fine narrative of the relationship between Hemingway and his editor, plus Fitzgerald and Thomas Wolfe.

Bruccoli, Matthew J. *Some Sort of Epic Grandeur: The Life of F. Scott Fitzgerald.* New York: Harcourt Brace

Jovanovich, 1981. Highly reliable Fitzgerald biography.

Bruccoli and Robert W. Trogdon, eds. *American Expatriate Writers: Paris in the Twenties* (*Dictionary of Literary Biography, Documentary Series,* 15). Detroit: Bruccoli Clark Layman / Gale, 1997.

Carr, Virginia Spencer. *Dos Passos: A Life.* Garden City: Doubleday, 1984.

Delaney, John, ed. *The House of Scribner, 1905–1936* (*Dictionary of Literary Biography, Documentary Series,* 16). Detroit: Bruccoli Clark Layman / Gale, 1997.

Diliberto, Gioia. *Hadley.* New York: Ticknor & Fields, 1992.

Donaldson, Scott. *Archibald MacLeish: An American Life.* Boston: Houghton Mifflin, 1992.

Ford, Hugh. *Published in Paris: A Literary Chronicle of Paris in the 1920s and 1930s.* New York: Macmillan, 1975.

Hansen, Arlen. *Expatriate Paris: A Cultural and Literary Guide to Paris of the 1920s.* New York: Little, Brown, 1990. The best of many street, place, and people guides to Paris in the 1920s.

Hoffman, Frederick. *The Twenties.* New York: Viking, 1955. Seminal cultural and literary survey of the era.

Ludington, Townsend. *John Dos Passos.* New York: E. P. Dutton, 1980.

Miller, Linda P. *Letters from the Lost Generation: Gerald and Sara Murphy and Friends.* New Brunswick, N.J.: Rutgers University Press, 1991.

Raeburn, John. *Fame Became of Him: Hemingway as a Public Writer.* Bloomington: Indiana University Press, 1984. Excellent documentation and analysis of Hemingway's rise to fame in the media.

Rollyson, Carl. *Nothing Ever Happens to the Brave: The Story of Martha Gellhorn.* St. Martin's Press, 1990. The unauthorized and only Gellhorn biography.

Rovit, Earl. *Ernest Hemingway.* New York: Twayne, 1963. Another seminal work that still makes sense.

Sarason, Bertram D. *Hemingway and the Sun Set.* Washington, D.C.: NCR Microcard Editions, 1972. Everything anyone ever wanted to know about the characters in *The Sun Also Rises,* with interviews.

Sokoloff, Alice H. *Hadley: The First Mrs. Hemingway.* New York: Dodd, Mead, 1973.

Stephens, Robert O. *Hemingway's Nonfiction.* Chapel Hill: University of North Carolina Press, 1968. First and best analysis of Hemingway's nonfiction and its relationship to his fiction.

Thomas, Hugh. *The Spanish Civil War.* New York: Harper & Row, 1961. Basic history.

Vaill, Amanda. *Everybody Was So Young: Gerald and Sara Murphy, a Lost Generation Love Story.* Boston: Houghton Mifflin, 1998.

Young, Philip. *Ernest Hemingway: A Reconsideration.* University Park: Pennsylvania State University Press, 1966. Along with Fenton and Baker, Young's book set the agenda for Hemingway criticism between 1955 and 1975.

PICTORIAL BIOGRAPHIES

Arnold, Lloyd. *Hemingway: High on the Wild.* New York: Grosset & Dunlap, 1977. Good source for photos of Hemingway in Idaho.

Buckley, Peter. *Ernest.* New York: Dial, 1978.

Fuentes, Norberto. *Ernest Hemingway Rediscovered.* New York: Scribners, 1988.

Gajdusek, Robert E. *Hemingway's Paris.* New York: Scribners, 1978.

Hotchner, A. E. *Hemingway and His World.* New York: Viking, 1989.

Trogdon, Robert W., ed., *Ernest Hemingway: A Documentary Volume* (*Dictionary of Literary Biography,* 210). Detroit: Bruccoli Clark Layman / Gale, 1999.

Voss, Frederick. *Picturing Hemingway.* New Haven: Yale University Press, 1999.

INTERNET RESOURCES

There are many online resources for Hemingway researchers and enthusiasts. Listed below are general sites of interest to students. Most contain links to other, more specialized, sites.

<http://www.hemingway.org/> Site maintained by the Hemingway Foundation to foster understanding of the life and work of Ernest Hemingway with emphasis on his Oak Park origins and his impact on world literature. Its mission reflects the Foundation's belief in the importance of the written word and the value of thoughtful reading and writing.

<http://www.atlantic.net/~gagne/hem/hem.html> Collection of general resources on Hemingway presented by the Department of English at the University of Florida.

<http://www.upnorth.net/hemingway/> Site maintained by the Michigan Hemingway Society—made up of university professors, writers, teachers, fly fishers, journalists and anyone interested in exploring Hemingway's work and its relationship to Michigan.

<http://www.lostgeneration.com/hrc.htm> General resources, featuring a biography, bibliography, audio clips, a writing contest, and a checklist of links.

MASTER INDEX

153

H

I

Venice, Italy 9, 79
Victory (Conrad) 131
Vidor, Charles 87
Viertel, Peter 88
Villon, François 136
Virgil 105
Vogel, Donald, Jr. 89
Vogue 60
"Voyage to Victory" (Hemingway) 8

W

Wain, John 106
Wallach, Eli 88
Walloon Lake, Michigan 2–3, 18–20, 22, 28, 72, 75, 120
War and Peace (Tolstoy) 105, 132
The Waste Land (Eliot) 35, 136
"A Way You'll Never Be" (Hemingway) 22, 61, 133, 135
Welles, Orson 87
Welsh, Mary. *See* Hemingway, Mary Welsh
The White Peacock (Lawrence) 100
White, Stewart Edward 131
White, William 63–64, 89
Wilder, Thornton 42
Williams, Tennessee 110

Wilson, Edmund 68
Winesburg, Ohio (Anderson) 105, 131
Winner Take Nothing (Hemingway) 6, 61, 67, 85
Wolfe, Thomas 6
Women in Love (Lawrence) 100
Wood, Sam 87
"The Woppian Way" (Hemingway) 3
World War I 1–2, 9, 30, 44, 55, 66, 77–78, 82, 132
World War II 1, 8–9, 11, 53–56, 63, 69, 89, 92, 97
Wuthering Heights (Brontë) 105
Wylder, Delbert 72

Y

Yeats, William Butler 89, 105, 107, 111
The Young Lions (Shaw) 57
Young, Philip 64, 70–71, 89

Z

Zanuck, Darryl F. 87